W9-BMJ-334

THE FATHERS
THE CHURCH

A NEW TRANSLATION

EDITORIAL BOARD

David G. Hunter
University of Kentucky
Editorial Director

drew Cain
sity of Colorado

Joseph T. Lienhard, S.J.
Fordham University

n Daley, S.J.
ity of Notre Dame

Rebecca Lyman
Church Divinity School of the Pacific

shbrook Harvey
n University

Wendy Mayer
Australian Catholic University

n E. Klingshirn
University of America

Robert D. Sider
Dickinson College

Trevor Lipscombe
Director
The Catholic University of America Press

FORMER EDITORIAL DIRECTORS

g Schopp, Roy J. Deferrari, Bernard M. Peebles,
ermigild Dressler, O.F.M., Thomas P. Halton

Carole Monica C. Burnett
Staff Editor

MUSKINGUM UNIVERSITY LIBRARY
163 STORMONT STREET
NEW CONCORD, OHIO 43762

THE F
OF THE   O

A NEW T

VOL

Uni

Br
Univer

Susan
Br

Willia
The Cathol

Lud

ST. CYRIL
OF ALEXANDRIA

THREE CHRISTOLOGICAL
TREATISES

Translated by

DANIEL KING

Cardiff University

THE CATHOLIC UNIVERSITY OF AMERICA PRESS
Washington, D.C.

Copyright © 2014
THE CATHOLIC UNIVERSITY OF AMERICA PRESS
All rights reserved
Printed in the United States of America

The paper used in this publication meets the minimum requirements of
the American National Standards for Information Science—Permanence
of Paper for Printed Library Materials, ANSI z39.48-1984.
∞

Library of Congress Cataloging-in-Publication Data
Cyril, Saint, Patriarch of Alexandria, approximately 370–444.
[Works. Selections. English]
Three Christological treatises / St. Cyril of Alexandria ;
translated by Daniel King.
pages cm.—(The Fathers of the Church,
a new translation ; volume 129)
Includes bibliographical references and indexes.
ISBN 978-0-8132-2705-4 (cloth : alk. paper)
1. Jesus Christ—Person and offices—Early works to 1800.
2. Jesus Christ—History of doctrines—Early church, ca. 30–600.
3. Theology, Doctrinal—History—Early church, ca. 30-600.
4. Nestorius, Patriarch of Constantinople, active 428.
I. King, Daniel, 1977–   II. Title.
BR65.C952E5 2014
232'.8–dc23
2014019388

CONTENTS

ABBREVIATIONS AND SIGLA

Abbreviations

ACO   Acta Conciliorum Oecumenicorum (Schwartz).

ANF   Ante-Nicene Fathers. 1890. Reprint. Grand Rapids: Eerdmans, 1994.

CSCO   Corpus Scriptorum Christianorum Orientalium.

FOTC   The Fathers of the Church. Washington, DC: The Catholic University of America Press.

LXX   Septuagint.

PG   Patrologia Graeca (ed. Migne).

SC   Sources chrétiennes. Paris: Cerf, 1941–.

Sigla

[ ]   Words inserted by the translator.

BIBLIOGRAPHY

Abramowski, L. "Zum Brief des Andreas von Samosata an Rabbula von Edessa." *Oriens Christianus* 41 (1957): 51–64.
———. "Peripatetisches bei späten Antiochenern." *Zeitschrift für Kirchengeschichte* 79 (1968): 358–62.
Boulnois, Marie-Odile. "L'eucharistie, mystère d'union chez Cyrille d'Alexandrie: les modèles d'union trinitaire et christologique." *Revue des sciences religieuses* 74 (2000): 147–72.
Burns, W. H., et al., eds. *Cyrille d'Alexandrie, Lettres Festales.* Sources chrétiennes 372. Paris: Éditions du Cerf, 1991.
Cassel, J. David. "Key Principles in Cyril of Alexandria's Exegesis." In *Studia patristica* 37. Edited by M. F. Wiles and E. J. Yarnold, with P. M. Parvis, 413–20. Leuven: Peeters, 2001.
Chadwick, H. "Florilegium." In *Reallexikon für Antike und Christentum,* edited by Theodore Klauser et al., col. 1131–60. Stuttgart: Anton Hiersemann, 1969.
Clayton, Paul B. *The Christology of Theodoret of Cyrus.* Oxford Early Christian Studies. Oxford: University Press, 2007.
Durand, G.-M. de, ed. *Deux dialogues christologiques.* Sources chrétiennes 97. Paris: Éditions du Cerf, 1964.
Galtier, P. "L' 'Unio secundum Hypostasim' chez Saint Cyrille." *Gregorianum* 33 (1952): 351–98.
———. "Saint Cyrille et Apollinaire." *Gregorianum* 37 (1956): 584–609.
Gray, P. T. R. *The Defense of Chalcedon in the East (451–553).* Leiden: Brill, 1979.
Guinot, J.-N. "L'exégèse de Cyrille d'Alexandrie et de Théodoret de Cyr: Un lieu de conflit ou de convergence?" *Cassiodorus* 4 (1998): 47–82.
———. *Théodoret de Cyr exégète et théologien. Un théologien engagé dans le conflit nestorien.* Paris: Éditions du Cerf, 2012.
King, Daniel. *The Syriac Versions of the Writings of Cyril of Alexandria: A Study in Translation Technique.* CSCO 626, Subsidia 123. Leuven: Peeters, 2008.
Lietzmann, H. *Apollinaris von Laodicea und seine Schule: Texte und Untersuchungen.* Tübingen, 1904.
Loofs, F. *Nestoriana. Die Fragmente des Nestorius.* Halle, 1905.
McGuckin, J. T. *St. Cyril of Alexandria: The Christological Controversy: Its*

History, Theology, and Texts. Supplements to *Vigiliae Christianae* 23. Leiden: Brill, 1994.

McKinion, S. A. *Words, Imagery, and the Mystery of Christ: A Reconstruction of Cyril of Alexandria's Christology.* Supplements to *Vigiliae Christianae* 55. Leiden: Brill, 2000.

O'Keefe, J. J. "Kenosis or Impassibility: Cyril of Alexandria and Theodoret of Cyrus on the Problem of Divine Pathos." In *Studia patristica* 32. Edited by E. A. Livingstone, 358–65. Leuven: Peeters, 1997.

Pásztori-Kupán, I. *Theodoret of Cyrus.* The Early Church Fathers. London and New York: Routledge, 2006.

Pericoli-Ridolfini, F. "Lettera Di Andrea Di Samosata a Rabbula Di Edessa." *Rivista degli Studi Orientali* 28 (1953): 153–69.

Pusey, Philip Edward. *Five Tomes against Nestorius: Scholia on the Incarnation; Christ Is One; Fragments against Diodore of Tarsus, Theodore of Mopsuestia, the Synousiasts.* Library of the Fathers of the Holy Catholic Church 47. Oxford, 1881.

Richard, M. "Les Florilèges Diphysites du Ve et du VIe siècle." In *Das Konzil von Chalkedon: Geschichte und Gegenwart,* edited by Alois Grillmeier and Heinrich Bacht, 721–43. Wurzburg: Echter-Verlag, 1951.

Russell, Norman. *Cyril of Alexandria.* Early Church Fathers. London and New York: Routledge, 2000.

Schwartz, E. *Acta conciliorum oecumenicorum.* Vols. I–IV. Berlin: De Gruyter, 1914–82.

Siddals, R. M. "Logic and Christology in Cyril of Alexandria." *Journal of Theological Studies* 38 (1987): 341–67.

Torrance, Iain R. *Christology after Chalcedon: Severus of Antioch and Sergius the Monophysite.* Norwich: Canterbury Press, 1988.

Vaccari, A. "La Grecità di S. Cirillo d'Alessandria." In *Studi dedicati alla memoria di Paolo Ubaldi,* edited by A. Gemelli, 27–39. Milan, 1937.

Weinandy, T., and D. A. Keating, eds. *The Theology of St. Cyril of Alexandria: A Critical Appreciation.* Edinburgh: T & T Clark, 2003.

Welch, L. J. "Logos-Sarx? Sarx and the Soul of Christ in the Early Thought of Cyril of Alexandria." *St. Vladimir's Theological Quarterly* 38.3 (1994): 271–92.

Wessel, Susan. *Cyril of Alexandria and the Nestorian Controversy: The Making of a Saint and of a Heretic.* Oxford Early Christian Studies. Oxford: University Press, 2004.

Wickham, L. R. *Cyril of Alexandria: Select Letters.* Oxford Early Christian Texts. Oxford: Clarendon Press, 1983.

INTRODUCTION

INTRODUCTION

The three works included in this volume all relate to Cyril of Alexandria's dispute with Nestorius, and later with other theologians, over the doctrine of the person of Christ. The first, *On Orthodoxy to Theodosius*,[1] a treatise addressed directly to the Emperor, was written in the early stages of the Nestorian controversy, probably in the summer of 430. The other two, both penned in the months preceding the third ecumenical council, which met at Ephesus at Pentecost 431, are defenses of his famous "twelve anathemas," which Cyril had used as a means to isolate Nestorius by outlawing those of his doctrines that Cyril deemed beyond the pale. One of these "defenses" is addressed specifically to Theodoret of Cyrus, the other to all the bishops of the diocese of Oriens.[2] The three texts together belong, therefore, to the story of how the Nestorian controversy developed from its early rumblings to the full-scale and dramatic confrontation that occurred at Ephesus, the long-term effects of which would be to rupture the worldwide church for good.

---

1. The full title is *logos prosphonêtikos pros ton eusebestaton basilea theodosion peri tês orthês pisteôs tês eis ton kurion hêmôn Iêsoun Christon* ("A Public Oration Addressed to the Most Pious King Theodosius concerning the Correct Faith that is in our Lord Jesus Christ").

2. The full titles of these works vary a great deal across the manuscripts. The first is entitled, in the oldest manuscript, *apologia pros tên para theodorêtou antirrêsin kata tôn dôdeka kephalaiôn* ("A Defense against the Refutation by Theodoret against the Twelve Chapters"). The second, in the Athenian manuscript, is called an *apologêtikos hyper tôn dôdeka kefalaiôn pros tous tês anatolês episkopous eggraphôs mempsamenous tois toioutois kephalaiois* ("A Defensive Work concerning the Twelve Chapters, against those Bishops of Oriens who were Critical of those same Chapters").

The Development of the Nestorian Controversy[3]

Cyril's own interaction with the teaching of Nestorius and the ruckus the latter was causing in the capital, especially his denial to the Virgin of the title "Mother-of-God," may be said to date from his seventeenth Paschal Letter, written for his own bishops and clergy for the Easter of 429 (approximately a year after Nestorius took office as bishop of Constantinople), and also from his extensive *Letter to the Monks* of his diocese, in which he found fault with many of Nestorius's published sermons.[4] Both of these early attacks on Nestorius were considered controversial, not only by the defendant himself but by many Antiochene bishops sympathetic to him. In his *Defense against the Bishops of Oriens,* Cyril needed to defend things he had written in both of these early skirmishes.

An increasingly polemical correspondence developed between the two bishops (Cyril's *First* and *Second Letters* together with Nestorius's replies to both),[5] and by the middle of 430 the stakes had risen and the highest authorities became involved. From a very early stage in the dispute Cyril maintained a close relationship with the Roman see, but he also saw the need to win the Emperor to his side; hence the first work in this vol-

---

3. The following narrative will confine itself to the specific concerns of our three treatises and will not needlessly repeat in detail the complex story of the build-up to the council, its progress, and outcome. Excellent and up-to-date summaries may be found in J. T. McGuckin, *St. Cyril of Alexandria: The Christological Controversy: Its History, Theology, and Texts,* Supplements to *Vigiliae Christianae* 23 (Leiden: Brill, 1994), 20–53, and Norman Russell, *Cyril of Alexandria,* Early Church Fathers (London and New York: Routledge, 2000), 31–39, as well as numerous other handbooks. Wessel includes a more in-depth look at some aspects of the events and texts concerned: Susan Wessel, *Cyril of Alexandria and the Nestorian Controversy: The Making of a Saint and of a Heretic,* Oxford Early Christian Studies (Oxford: University Press, 2004).

4. The Paschal letter has been edited and translated in *Cyrille d'Alexandrie, Lettres Festales Tome III,* ed. W. H. Burns, trans. M.-O. Boulnois and B. Meurnier, Sources chrétiennes 434 (Paris: Éditions du Cerf, 1998). See also FOTC 127, trans. Amidon and O'Keefe. The *Letter to the Monks* became the opening item in the official dossier arising from the Council of Ephesus and is therefore numbered *Ep.* 1 in Cyril's published correspondence. Text in *Acta Conciliorum Oecumenicorum* (ACO) 1.1.1, pp. 10–23; translation in McGuckin, 245–61.

5. Translations in McGuckin, 262–75.

ume, *On Orthodoxy to Theodosius*. In this his first missive to the court on the subject, Cyril diplomatically avoids so much as mentioning the person of the bishop of Constantinople himself, even though he was simultaneously composing his five-volume point-by-point dismantling of Nestorius's sermons.[6] The treatise was sent to the Emperor in the company of two others, known respectively as *On Orthodoxy to the Empresses* (addressed to Pulcheria and Eudocia, the Emperor's sister and wife) and as *On Orthodoxy to the Princesses* (addressed to his two younger sisters, Arcadia and Marina). It was the letter addressed to the Emperor, however, that he believed would prove the most crucial for attempting to secure his own cause (an aim in which it was not wholly successful). This letter is sufficient for giving the reader a sense both of how far Cyril's attack on "Nestorianism" had progressed at this early stage of the dispute and also of the political strategy he was adopting as a means to win that dispute at the highest level.

The major event that separates these addresses to the court from the far more direct and confrontational texts written in the autumn and winter of 430/1 was the active intervention of the pope. The results of Cyril's approach to the Roman see were far swifter and more congenial than the response he received from the imperial court. The controversy that formed the jumping-off point for *On Orthodoxy* moved up a gear when Pope Celestine decided against Nestorius and demanded that he recant his position. Cyril was emboldened to compose his famous twelve propositions, framed as anathemas, designed specifically to prevent either Nestorius or his sympathizers from hiding behind vague verbal agreements that adhered to the creeds only in name. These anathemas were appended to Cyril's *Third Letter to Nestorius*.

While it had been only a question of debating the use of the term "Mother-of-God," John of Antioch and his bishops of the

6. *Five Tomes against Nestorius.* A full translation may be found in Philip Edward Pusey, *Five Tomes against Nestorius: Scholia on the Incarnation; Christ Is One; Fragments against Diodore of Tarsus, Theodore of Mopsuestia, the Synousiasts,* Library of the Fathers of the Holy Catholic Church 47 (Oxford, 1881); extensive extracts in Russell, *Cyril of Alexandria.*

diocese of Oriens had been so far content to persuade Nestorius to agree (and we shall see that Theodoret does not oppose the use of the title), but the anathemas were bound to alienate many more and, if driven home, would probably have excommunicated half the church! It was these bishops, rather than the previously isolated Nestorius, who quickly became, even before the council, the main focus of Cyril's writings. The whole axis of the controversy was about to shift to a battle between the theological heavyweights of the day, Cyril and Theodoret.

Hence it was between Nestorius's reception of the infamous *Third Letter* in December 430 and the gathering of the Council of Ephesus at Pentecost (June 7th) 431 that Cyril was forced to defend his anathemas against the many bishops throughout the eastern provinces who found them too extreme in their denunciation of Nestorius's way of expressing the union of the natures in Christ. In the eyes of many sympathizers, Nestorius was simply repeating the teaching of his master Chrysostom and the other theologians of the Antiochene tradition. On the other hand, they objected to the strongly paradoxical statements of incarnational theology that Cyril used, most prominently the radical proclamation that "God died in the flesh."

It was John of Antioch, as primate of the see of Oriens,[7] who quite naturally took the lead in responding negatively to the anathemas, but a small coterie of subordinate bishops formed the backbone of the opposition—Alexander of Hierapolis, who would later retain his hardline, anti-Cyril position in the face of the post-Ephesus reconciliation; Theodoret of Cyrus, who was growing in stature to become one of the leading lights of Christian theology in that part of the world; and Andrew of Samosata, one of the most senior bishops that John could call upon. Both Andrew and Theodoret wrote refutations of the anathemas at John's request.[8] They must have done their work speedi-

7. It should be borne in mind that when Cyril speaks of "Oriental" bishops, this is a neutral and quite specific term for referring to the bishops of the diocese of *Oriens* under the leadership of John of Antioch, just as his own subordinates would be called the Egyptian bishops.

8. In Theodoret's letter to John (*Ep.* 150), translated below as a preface to his refutation, the bishop describes his own initial, shocked reaction to reading the anathemas and the bishop of Antioch's request for him to write a response.

ly, for Cyril had time both to receive copies of these refutations and to write his counter-refutations within the space of the six months that separated the publication of the anathemas themselves from the council. This is a testimony, of course, to the importance Cyril attached to this particular source of opposition. His dismissive polemics against Theodoret and Andrew belie an acknowledgment of the force of the Antiochene response and his realization that the moment of truth was fast approaching, when the future direction of Christendom would be decided by those who could persuade the Emperor of the righteousness of their cause.

A copy of Theodoret's work (probably "leaked" by the author himself) fell into the hands of Cyril's ally the bishop of Ptolemais and metropolitan of the Pentapolis (Upper Libya), Euoptius. If, as seems likely, this man was the brother of Synesius, the former bishop of Ptolemais, then he was certainly a useful friend for Cyril. As a former student of Hypatia in Alexandria, a highly educated and well-connected aristocrat, Euoptius was to become one of Cyril's key supporters over the coming months. Euoptius passed Theodoret's work on to Alexandria, and Cyril's response (translated here) gives some indication, if rather overblown, of the latter's feelings on first seeing these accusations against him written by the only other theologian of his time who could do real damage to his future prospects.

Theodoret is a well-known figure of church history, and the interested reader may safely be directed elsewhere for an account of his life and works.[9] By comparison with those of his much better known colleague, however, Andrew of Samosata's extant works are rather thin on the ground. Besides a number of brief letters to his colleagues (found in the Collectio Casinensis),[10] the main texts from his pen are the letter to Rabbula of Edessa and two separate refutations of Cyril's anathemas.[11] The first of these

9. A good recent work on Theodoret's Christology is Paul B. Clayton, *The Christology of Theodoret of Cyrus*, Oxford Early Christian Studies (Oxford: University Press, 2007).

10. Details may be found in the *Clavis Patrum Graecorum*.

11. The letter was only preserved in a Syriac version, although it is also possible that it was written in Syriac, since both writer and addressee were bilinguals. For the letter, see F. Pericoli-Ridolfini, "Lettera Di Andrea Di Samosata a

refutations was the one to which Cyril responded in the text here translated; the other, written perhaps shortly after the Council, is extant only in a short extract relating to the fourth anathema embedded in a work by Anastasius of Sinai.[12] In this latter work, Andrew launches a more wide-ranging offensive against the anathemas, quoting Cyril against himself and demonstrating the dissonance between the Alexandrian's terminology as applied to anti-Arian Trinitarian thought and as applied to Christology.

Andrew's refutation was composed in the name of all the bishops of Oriens, that is, as under commission from John of Antioch himself. It can thus be taken as to some extent the "official" position of the Antiochenes. This distinguishes it from Theodoret's attack, which was the result more of personal repulsion (though also written at John's request) and which only reached Cyril via unofficial channels. As far as one can tell from the fragments extant in Cyril's reply, Andrew's version was the less polemical and provocative, though it is hardly conciliatory. It aimed to bring to the surface contradictions in Cyril's own writings and thereby to demonstrate that the anathemas are not really the summary of Alexandrian theology that they purport to be. The intention may have been to distance Cyril from his own bishops by making the former seem extreme even by the standards of his own tradition.

Cyril thus spent the early months of 431, before the ecumenical council was due to meet in June, composing his replies to these two attacks. The works belong to the cut-and-thrust of controversy rather than to the more lackadaisical style of theological reflection found in some of Cyril's writings. There was, in any case, always more in Cyril of the politician and the demagogue than of the philosopher. This does not mean, of course, that his theology is in any way insincere. It was the error of Gibbon, and of many since, to think that Cyril's grating style and sometimes vicious polemic, combined with his underhanded

---

Rabbula Di Edessa," *Rivista degli Studi Orientali* 28 (1953): 153–69. See the two important articles by L. Abramowski: "Zum Brief des Andreas von Samosata an Rabbula von Edessa," *Oriens Christianus* 41 (1957): 51–64, and "Peripatetisches bei späten Antiochenern," *Zeitschrift für Kirchengeschichte* 79 (1968): 358–62.

12. The Greek text is most easily found in the *Patrologia Graeca* or in Abramowski (1957), 55–57.

machinations at court and liberal use of bribery, should be taken to imply that his motivations had more to do with the power of his episcopal throne than with Christian thinking. Both are western and orientalizing suspicions. On the contrary, the sense one receives from reading these works is of a man who is (over) sure of being in the right, but whose assurance arises from a keen intellect driven towards what he sees as vital truths that need to be maintained at all costs.

What makes all three works so valuable, then, is the window that they offer into Cyril's thinking at these two slightly different points in the story: one before the anathemas were written and before Celestine's support was secured, when the bishop of Alexandria was still feeling his way into the dispute; the other after the anathemas and the escalation of the conflict but still before the council itself had taken place. The work *On Orthodoxy to Theodosius* is general and wide-ranging and seeks to establish the bounds of orthodoxy. It avoids naming names or making accusations against living persons. The two *Apologies* show us Cyril in the thick of battle, with his impassioned *ad hominem* arguments and gritty defensiveness at the accusations to which he has just been subjected. It was perhaps only when he first read Theodoret's refutation of the anathemas that Cyril finally realized that he had a genuine fight on his hands against an intellectual heavyweight and that he would need every ounce of theological *nous* and rhetorical strategy to win the day.

Theological Summaries of the Texts

1. On Orthodoxy to Theodosius

Cyril opens his address to Theodosius with a fawning discourse on the quasi-divine status and role of emperors,[13] exhorting him to stay true to his role as guardian of Christian doctrine by comparing him to King Hezekiah of Judah, who did away with "heresy" in his kingdom.

---

13. Two are mentioned since, officially at least, the western Emperor Valentinian III was an equal partner with Theodosius, though this fiction was not maintained for long.

With these introductory pleasantries out of the way, Cyril begins his discussion proper (ch. 6), a summary version of the teachings of six Christological heresies—Docetism, theomorphism, Arianism, adoptionism, Apollinarianism, and finally dyophysitism. Cyril's rhetorical *coup de grâce*, of course, is to make Nestorius's doctrine the last of these enemies of the true church (and therefore the most recent as well as perhaps the most heinous). He describes this heresy by quoting from Nestorius's sermons without actually naming the bishop himself and so "constructs" Nestorianism before the fact. Instead of defending himself against his opponent from the dock,[14] Cyril puts himself into the judge's seat. He defines orthodox belief and allows the Emperor to come to "his own" conclusions.

In this "prelude," then, Cyril constructs the semi-fiction that his work is some sort of exhaustive heresiology. It is clear from the increasing amount of space devoted to each heresy, however, that the first four are not the point of the treatise—they are there to show Cyril to be the constructor of orthodoxy. His ability to refute heresy establishes his credentials as a theologian and locates Cyril himself at the end of the historical stream of orthodox bishops. This catalogue of historical errors enables him properly to exclude himself from any association with them (Docetism, theomorphism, and Apollinarianism were all errors attributed to him by opponents) and to place dyophysitism in turn within a "history of heresy."

The first of the heresies described (chs. 7–9) is Docetism. The belief that the Word of God became man only in appearance was one of the oldest forms of "heterodox" opinion, traditionally associated with Valentinus and other "gnostic" groups. Its refutation was the stock-in-trade of many pre-Nicene theologians (Ignatius, Irenaeus, Hippolytus, Tertullian).[15]

Although Docetism is hardly Cyril's principal target, it offers

14. Recall that Nestorius planned to organize a synod to condemn Cyril.

15. E.g., see Iren., *haer.* 3.9.3, for a basic statement of the counter-argument, the similarity of which to Cyril's is immediately obvious; also 3.11.3; 4.6.7. For Hippolytus, *haer.* 8.1–4; 10.12. Tertullian attacks the doctrine especially as being that of Marcion, e.g., *Adv. Marc.* 4.8; 4.40; he also wrote a treatise particularly dealing with it, the *De carne Christi.*

him an opportunity to state his own Christological position,[16] and he did feel pressured to demonstrate the radical difference between it and his own position. Cyril's attack revolves around the argument from soteriology—that is, if Christ only "seemed" to be the Word of God incarnate, then "[t]he fact of his being 'with us' would mean nothing at all" (ch. 9). For salvation to be real, for the Eucharist to be a genuine channel of redemption, all the sufferings of Christ must also be real and physical.[17] The efficacy of liturgy and Eucharist was ever an especial concern of the Alexandrian tradition.[18] Cyril's theology of the single-subject flesh incarnate was always open to accusations of docetic tendencies, as would become apparent when Eutyches claimed Cyril's authority in his extreme version of monophysitism at the "Robber Council" at Ephesus (449).

The second heresy is, in some sense, the opposite of Docetism. It is the belief that in the Incarnation the Word of God *changed* from being divine into being flesh. The source for this passage is Athanasius's refutation of theomorphism in his letter to Epictetus (*Ep.* 54),[19] a text with which Cyril frequently aligns himself (cf. Cyril's *Ep.* 40.21) and which became a key patristic witness at subsequent councils.[20]

16. He quotes 1 Tm 3.16 to support a classic Cyrillian formulation, namely, that the very Word of God the Father "was manifest in the flesh," and he makes early use of the title *Theotokos*, Mother-of-God, the honorific title that Nestorius and his lackeys were trying to deny her.

17. This use of the soteriological argument in Christology goes back to Irenaeus and Novatian, e.g., Iren., *haer.* 5.14.2–4; Nov., *trin.* 10: "nor can we perceive any salvation of ours in him, if in him we do not even recognize the salvation of our body" (trans. Ernest Wallis, ANF 5, p. 619). Cyril is dependent upon Athanasius for his use of the Epistle to the Hebrews in support of this line of argument; compare the former's *Letter to Epictetus* 5 with Cyril's *On Orthodoxy* 8.4.

18. Marie-Odile Boulnois, "L'eucharistie, mystère d'union chez Cyrille d'Alexandrie: les modèles d'union trinitaire et christologique," *Revue des sciences religieuses* 74 (2000): 147–72.

19. Cyril summed up "theomorphism" as the belief that the Word "was changed into a nature of bones, nerves and flesh," a quotation from *ep. epict.* 4. Both texts make use in particular of Is 50.6.

20. The letter's formulae became the basis upon which Cyril and the Oriental bishops could be reconciled in 433. Its manuscript transmission was closely bound up with Cyril's Christological letters.

The discussion facilitates Cyril's construction of a "history of heresy" while simultaneously offering him a chance to cut off possible avenues of criticism. As we shall see in the refutations of the anathemas, Cyril's own position was viewed by some as being of this sort. For these opponents, talk about the "single incarnate nature of the Word" must imply some form of (unthinkable) substantial transformation within the godhead, what Theodoret would call a literal "becoming."

Next up is the "adoptionism" of Marcellus of Ancyra and Photinus of Sirmium, who are explicitly named (ch. 6), although the term "adoptionism" is not used, nor is its prototypical exponent, Paul of Samosata, mentioned. Marcellus was a famous antagonist of Arius who perceived the underlying problem with Arianism in Christological terms, namely, that its root error was its "word-flesh" type of understanding of the person of Christ. By opposing to this a more radical differential between Word and Man in Christ, Marcellus hoped to undermine the Arian subordination of the Son in relation to the Trinity. He moved so far in this direction, however, that he became "guilty" of the heresy of Paul of Samosata. Photinus was an even more extreme case of the same tendency. He was accused of treating Christ as a "mere man," an accusation that Cyril will often throw at Nestorius.

In a sense Cyril is here launching a first attack against Antiochene theology more generally, for when the Alexandrians combatted Arianism they did so by denying that everything predicated of the Word must be so according to his "divine nature," and hence they sought to preserve the inviolability of that nature, a position that ends by supposing that a special state (incarnate-ness) is attributable to the nature of the Logos (what Theodoret would call attributing change to the godhead). Antiochenes such as Marcellus, on the other hand, tried to dissolve Arius's unitive understanding of Christ as a way of undercutting his argument for the Son's subordination, the result being a division of the experiences of Christ between the two natures (what Cyril would call a doctrine of two sons). When in later years Cyril would write against Theodore and Diodore, he would be thinking of them as pseudo-Marcelluses.

Apollinarianism (chs. 16–24) receives considerably more extended treatment. The accusation of Apollinarian tendencies was ever at Cyril's door, and, as is now well known, a number of Apollinarian formulae (albeit under "orthodox" names) are favorably cited by Cyril and even used as fundamental patristic testimony. Nonetheless, Apollinarianism is formally rejected as a form of Docetism, a doctrine that offers no salvation because the Word does not become a true human and does not fully participate in human nature (ch. 19). Cyril insists that true Christianity requires a Christ who functions fully as a human even when he descended into hell (ch. 22), and he concludes with a resounding affirmation of his own supposedly completely non-Apollinarian position (ch. 24). It is notable and significant, however, that Cyril always favors the creeds of the church over philosophical proof, and even where he openly sees the force of the Apollinarian argument, prefers to reside in the safety of the tradition (ch. 17).

It comes as no surprise that the longest section of the treatise (chs. 25–45) is devoted to dyophysitism, to those who "divide the single Christ into two ... and so represent each one of them as having a separate existence. They maintain that one of these parts is completely human and was born of a virgin, while the other one is the Word of God the Father" (ch. 6). The key to Nestorius's error, as Cyril sees it, is that it introduces two subject-centers in Christ, two consciousnesses, each of which is allowed to "stand on its own terms" (*ana meros*). Many of the criticisms of this doctrine that he makes here in the treatise addressed to Theodosius would soon reappear in the twelve anathemas, for example, against the language of appropriation as opposed to the language of incarnation; against the notion that the human part of Christ may receive the title of "son" only by association; and against the idea of attributing Jesus's sayings to either "the god alone" or "the man alone."

The theological content of this section will be familiar enough from any summary of Cyril's Christology. He stresses as always the incoherence of a two-subject Christology with the biblical and patristic testimonies. Although he acknowledges that the term "firstborn" refers to Christ in his human aspect while the title

"Only-Begotten" refers to the divine aspect, both are so wholly a single subject that either element may be described as the object of genuine worship; that is, there can only be one active subject in Christ just as there can only be one object of worship in Christ (ch. 30). The unity in Christ is so total that worship may be offered under either name (ch. 32). Hence the soul/body analogy gets trotted out in this context (ch. 34), and leads Cyril into one of his disquisitions upon the Eucharist (ch. 38), the efficacy of which is ensured only by a genuine and total union, a single-subject Christology. The final few chapters contain a number of extended exegeses, mostly from John's gospel, which were developed during Cyril's years as a detailed commentator and here are put to good polemical use.

What really matters to Cyril above all in *On Orthodoxy*, however, is maintaining his consistency with the patristic tradition. The battle over doctrine is in fact a battle over the ownership of tradition. "Those who separate out the parts and divide them up," he says, "cannot manage it at all, whereas for those who bind Emmanuel together into a unity, the pure knowledge of the holy doctrines is readily comprehensible." In other words, the dogmatic formula to be accepted is the one that sits most easily with the patristic tradition. A genuine sea-change is observable here in the methods and expectations of theological debate, and the shift from biblical to patristic authority as the touchstone of orthodoxy is already underway. These changes are even more apparent in Cyril's defenses against Theodoret and the bishops of Oriens.

2. The Defenses of the Twelve Anathemas

As one reads through Cyril's ripostes to Andrew and Theodoret, what strikes the reader repeatedly is the series of firmly held premises that control and co-ordinate everything Cyril says and writes: that salvation is of purely divine origin, that it was brought to man by a genuine incarnation, a real en-fleshment of the Word of God, and that it is this process that is realized in the individual by the presence of God in Christ within the sacraments of the church. Anything that seems to endanger this basic central structure, or that might do so if taken to its logical conclusion, is deemed beyond the pale. So absolute is the effect of the real union between God and man, without which human salvation is an ephemeral hope, that he can not only say, as he does in the final anathema, that "God suffered," but also can exclude from Christian communion any who refuse to agree. Cyril is clearly a man on a mission.

But what of the arguments themselves with which Theodoret and Andrew attack the anathemas? Any reader seeking profound consideration of the issues or philosophically nuanced rebuttals of the anathemas will probably be disappointed. In this, the very earliest of the sparring matches between Cyril and his Antiochene opponents, the degree of mutual understanding is slight, and Theodoret in particular, perhaps genuinely taken aback by the rhetorical forcefulness of the anathemas, does not seem to have delved into the real theological concerns that lie behind them. None of the parties engage in any in-depth analysis of the fundamental terminology that they are using. The objections often come across as rather weak, and in fact Cyril leaps upon the slightest such weakness with the eagerness of a lioness devouring an easy kill.

In reality both participants are using arguments of the type, "If you say *x*, this will lead inevitably to *y*, which is clearly unacceptable even on your own premises," and the response usually comes back, "You misunderstand what *x* means, and it certainly does not lead to *y*." In other words, what is happening here is that these two rigorous theologians are encountering one another's formulae and terminology for the first time, sounding them out for hollow spots and weaknesses, and offering arguments as to why his own are preferable, even if the opponent's are not wholly objectionable. This, in fact, is the position that both sides eventually reached by 433, still attached to their different modes of expression and yet willing to allow the other's to carry on unmolested if properly understood.

First anathema: that Mary is the "Mother-of-God" because she bore Christ "in the flesh" (*kata sarka*).

Andrew and Theodoret focus their objections upon the expression "in the flesh." To them this implies transformation of the divine nature, and both suggest that the expression "he dwelt among us" would be more appropriate, or "fitting to God" (*theoprepês*). Following Philippians 2.7, Theodoret prefers the expression "he took flesh upon himself," though he is quite willing on this basis to bestow upon the Virgin the title "Mother-of-God," an important departure from Nestorius's hardline position, which had actually precipitated the crisis in the first place. His logic is this: if what was born was begotten of the Holy Spirit (Matthew 1.23), then it was a creation of the Spirit and cannot be equated with the pre-existent Word; it must refer to the "form of the servant" alone.

Cyril is at his most aggressive when he feels unfairly accused of taking a position that he despises; hence his dismissal of Theodoret's suggestion that his own doctrine implies change in the godhead.[21] His own doctrine implies no such thing (he argues) whereas a language of "taking" such as Theodoret prefers offers no genuine incarnation. Calling Mary the "Mother-of-the-Man," as Nestorius had, was tantamount to making Christ no better than a saint. In responding to Andrew, Cyril makes rather more of Nestorius's own shortcomings and attempts to reveal the faulty workings of his logic. As so often in these debates, the effort is focused on showing that one particular formulation necessarily gives rise to a position which all parties would agree to be heretical. Nestorius argued that the title "Mother-of-God" must imply change in the divine nature. Not at all, replies Cyril. In fact, one cannot help but qualify the Nativity with the expression "in the flesh" unless intending to deny that the one who was born was really the Word at all—and so Cyril too is using the same form of argument as Nestorius and his advocates.

For Cyril, the expression "incarnate" is no metaphor and is therefore not equivalent to calling the Word a "sin and a curse" (one of Andrew's arguments). It was used by the Fathers and is, for that reason alone, to be taken seriously and literally. There is no need to say that the Magi offered gifts both to a visible child and to an invisible Word—there was only a single

---

21. Note that Cyril had already discussed this doctrine in the early chapters of *On Orthodoxy to Theodosius*, presumably for this very reason.

incarnate Word, a genuine unity of personhood. The relevant expressions, "in the flesh" and "according to flesh," are strictly synonyms, and the orthodox Fathers used these expressions in reference to the birth of Christ.

Cyril's citations from both Alexandrian and Antiochene Fathers, in his response to the Oriental bishops, is an example of his new departure in theological method. The technique of quoting the works of the Fathers as evidence was used only sparingly before the Nestorian controversy. It was to be used in the dossiers prepared for Ephesus with devastating effect and became a cornerstone of theological method thereafter among both pro- and anti-Chalcedonians.[22]

Second anathema: that the union occurred at the level of concrete existence (*kath' hypostasin*), yielding a single individual or subject (*ton auton*).

To unite things "at the level of concrete existence" entails mixture (*krasis*) and hence confusion (*sugchusis*), argues Theodoret (no response to this anathema has been preserved from Andrew). In a true mixture, the properties of the original ingredients are lost, and this is ruled out in the case of the incarnate Word.

In amidst the harsh polemical tone of his response, Cyril's strategy is again simple: to expose the logic of Theodoret's position and to deny its coherence. Quite simply, the expression "at the level of concrete existence" is the only way to fend off extreme Nestorian divisions and in no way entails mixture (let alone confusion).

In this rhetorically charged atmosphere, the use of the terms mixture (*krasis*) and confusion (*sugchusis*) is imprecise. In both Aristotelian and Stoic terminology, mixture and confusion are

---

22. M. Richard, "Les Florilèges Diphysites du Ve et du VIe siècle," in *Das Konzil von Chalkedon: Geschichte und Gegenwart,* ed. Alois Grillmeier and Heinrich Bacht, 721–43 (Würzburg: Echter-Verlag, 1951); H. Chadwick, "Florilegium," in *Reallexikon für Antike und Christentum,* ed. Theodore Klauser et al., col. 1131–60 (Stuttgart: Anton Hiersemann, 1969); P. T. R. Gray, *The Defense of Chalcedon in the East (451–553)* (Leiden: Brill, 1979); Daniel King, *The Syriac Versions of the Writings of Cyril of Alexandria: A Study in Translation Technique,* CSCO 626, Subsidia 123 (Leuven: Peeters, 2008), 4–11.

separate categories of combinations. The Aristotelian "mixture" did, in fact, offer a useful description of the Incarnation since its whole aim is to preserve the properties of the individual ingredients by suggesting that they continue to exist within the mixture "in potentiality."[23] Many previous theologians had used the term freely,[24] although Theodoret's suspicion of it, and his equating it with "confusion," was a common theme in the Antiochene tradition.[25] In his recently written work against Nestorius, Cyril had explained the term away as a "loose usage" among the Fathers;[26] hence he seeks neither to defend it nor to distinguish it sharply from "confusion," but rather hopes to show that a union "at the level of concrete existence" implies no more than a single-subject result. How this is *not* a mixture of some sort he does not attempt to show, and it would perhaps have been difficult for him to do so.

Third anathema: that the convergence ("connection" is an inappropriate term) of human and divine in the one Christ is now asserted to be not merely at the level of concrete existence but equally "at the level of a natural union" (*kath' henôsin phusikên*).

Theodoret finds the distinction between "connection" and "convergence" meaningless and continues to accuse Cyril of covering up for a mixture-Christology. Both he and Andrew also claim not to comprehend Cyril's insistence on qualifying the union as "natural"; to them this seems equivalent to "involuntary." Andrew also quotes Cyril against himself from an earlier letter to the effect that the divinity has its own special nature (and by extension so does the humanity) and hence the union could not be at the level of "nature."[27]

Cyril's response to Theodoret focuses on defending the term

---

23. For Aristotle's account of mixture, *De generatione et corruptione* 1.10.

24. E.g., Gregory of Nazianzus, *Or.* 38.13.

25. Theodore of Mopsuestia, *fr. inc.* (PG 66:981A).

26. *Five Tomes against Nestorius* 1.3.

27. The technique of citing discrepancies within the writings of Cyril was to remain a common sport among theologians of all traditions over the following centuries. It is undoubtedly true that Cyril grew more cautious and precise in his formulations as the controversy developed, although he never made this point in his own defense.

"natural" as equivalent to "genuine" and meaning nothing more than that. Theodoret's argument that "natural" meant "involuntary" is reduced to an absurdity. Cyril's strategy is to isolate his opponent as the one who uses language in a strange way, while he himself uses it in its "everyday" sense ("apparently *he* is the only one who knows what absolutely everybody knows").[28] The important distinction is stressed between the time *before* the union, when our minds can conceive that there were two quite distinct natures, and the time *after* the union, when any talk of division is both unscriptural and logically dangerous. This latter point is driven home against Andrew as well, but not before he has used the opportunity to quote a sermon from Nestorius that explicitly speaks of "dividing the natures." For Cyril, this is a foil to explain why his anathema is so timely and necessary.[29] Neither Andrew nor Theodoret expresses himself as strongly as Nestorius did, but formulae such as "I divide the natures but unite the worship" went back to Diodore and hence constituted a weak point in the Antiochene armor. Finally, a disclaimer is added regarding Apollinarius, who is mentioned by name in Andrew's critique, not so much for his Christology as for his objectionable millennialism, which is as arbitrary and irrational as Cyril's Christology.

Fourth anathema: that the well-worn exegetical procedure of parceling out the actions and words of Jesus to the two natures involves an unacceptable degree of division; all of these things must be predicated of the single subject, the incarnate Word.

Both of Cyril's opponents focus on criticizing the extremeness of his position. Andrew appears the more defensive. He affirms the idea of single-subject predication in general, and is in fact very careful not to concede this ground wholly to the Alexandrian, but he is unwilling to give up the balancing idea that one can (and must) perceive different subjects for different ac-

28. In Cyril's defense of the third anathema in *A Defense of the Twelve Anathemas against Theodoret.*

29. He is here drawing directly on material prepared at greater length for his *Five Tomes against Nestorius,* which were probably composed simultaneously with, or shortly before, these treatises.

tions. This is needed, he says, to keep Arians and Eunomians at bay. These heretics had assumed that everything Christ did and said was done by one subject and thereby "introduce[d] human baseness into the transcendent nature."[30] Here is a truly sore point for Cyril, and it is one that Theodoret pounces on. After all, it was to be the charge of Arianism that would bring about Cyril's fall in the early stages of the Council of Ephesus. When John of Antioch and Theodoret attempt to justify to Rome their action in deposing Cyril, they refer in particular to the horror caused by this anathema:

He even anathematizes those who make distinctions among the expressions used by the apostles and evangelists about the Lord Christ, people who attribute expressions of a more humble nature to [Christ's] humanity, and to Christ's divinity those that are more appropriate to God. It is with these views that Arians and Eunomians attributed the expressions of a humble nature, concerning the plan of salvation, to the divinity and so were brazen enough to claim that God the Word had been made and created, that he was of a different substance than the Father's, that they were unlike each other.[31]

The charge of holding an Arian Christology had to be handled delicately, and Cyril shows a flexibility at this point rarely found elsewhere. Whereas the anathema certainly seems, on first reading, to dismiss all distinctions between different dominical sayings, Cyril now insists that he never intended there to be no distinction at all, but merely to insist on there being a single subject of all of them. The anathemas were not designed (he says) as a full statement of his own theology but as a series of assertions whose purpose was to coax Nestorius's position into the open. This must be borne in mind when they are read on their own or out of context.

Fifth anathema: that the expression "god-bearing man" (*theophoros anthrôpos*) is incompatible with the notion that Christ was genuinely one with the Word.

No response from Andrew has been preserved for the fifth or sixth anathemas. To Cyril's anathematization of the term

30. See the Orientals' critique of the fourth anathema in *A Defense of the Twelve Anathemas against the Bishops of the Diocese of Oriens.*

31. ACO 1.1.3, p. 41, 9–16 (Theodoret, *ep.* 170).

"god-bearing man," Theodoret objects that the expression is found in Basil of Caesarea; hence we see an early instance of patristic authority being contested. Cyril sidesteps this particular problem (in fact Theodoret's allusion does not wholly support his case) and refocuses instead on refuting the accusation that his doctrine entails change in the godhead, referring back to arguments made under the first anathema.

Sixth anathema: that the Word was not the "God of Christ"; this expression also implies a dual subject.

Theodoret again tries to pinpoint the principal area of disagreement. He does not rise to the bait of calling the Word the "God of Christ," but he continues to argue that the term "servant" (in the sense of Philippians 2.7) is still applicable to Christ after the union, and was so applied by the apostles; hence what was formed in the womb can be said to have been the "servant," but not "the Word."

Now Cyril need not disagree about the apostolic usage. After all, Cyril's doctrine has no problem in assimilating apostolic expressions that are human-oriented rather than divinely oriented. What is politically significant, however—and this was perhaps Theodoret's blunder—is that Nestorius had described the relationship between Word and Christ in the manner set out in the anathema. And yet Theodoret has failed fully to defend him when he had the chance. Cyril pounces on the omission, sensing (not without reason) that Theodoret will not really defend Nestorius to the bitter end and may be forced to admit the point of the anathema. This is Cyril's "divide-and-rule" strategy against the Antiochenes.

Seventh anathema: that if one says that the miracles and deeds of Christ were carried out by the Word in the same way that one might say that he acts within a holy man, this is again tantamount to a two-subject Christology.

Theodoret quotes Paul to defend the anathematized notion of God "working within" the human Christ and thereby glorifying him with the Son's glory. Andrew uses the same Pauline verse (Ephesians 1.19–20) and, as is his wont, takes care to defend his position from being taken to mean that Christ was no more than a great prophet. But Cyril sees it quite the other way around. The miracles were not cases of the glorification of a human being but of God the Word directly revealing himself in an incarnate state to human beings. Again, Cyril can easily point to quotations from Nestorius that are clearly more extreme than anything Andrew or Theodoret would want to say, and Cyril will not tire of pointing it out.

Eighth anathema: that the dual worship prescribed by Nestorius is a clear case of a dualist Christology rather than a genuine union, and is unacceptable.

Again Andrew will not go so far as Nestorius in demanding a double act of worship, and hence he is essentially in agreement with the anathema, albeit he does complain of Cyril's pedantry at the term "together with," which he believes he can detect in some of Cyril's earlier writings. Theodoret too is somewhat defensive at this point and insists that he too offers a single act of worship.

It is here that Cyril famously quotes Apollinarius under the name of Athanasius, whence the soon-to-be-infamous expression, "one incarnate nature of the Word." There can be no doubt that Cyril was as deceived as anyone. But was he really, as Theodoret and Andrew certainly assume throughout their refutations, an Apollinarian? The most truthful answer is probably that, to a degree, he was. For the modern reader, it is hardly a criminal charge, and one may choose to congratulate Cyril on unknowingly canonizing the thoughts of an excellent theologian who had a genuine contribution to make. If certain parts of Apollinarius's position may indeed be deemed fruitful and valid, then the accusation may actually bolster Cyril's by association. Apollinarius was one of the most astute Christological thinkers in the early church who proposed a series of measures designed to establish a logically coherent doctrine in the face of the increasingly disparate and politically motivated formulae of the councils. Cyril famously latched on to Apollinarius's expression, "one incarnate nature of the Word," thinking it to have been penned by Athanasius, but although the revelation of its true provenance may have been a scandal to his followers, it need be so no longer.

Ninth anathema: that Christ's miracle-working was an outwork-ing of his own power rather than being a faculty that he derived from the Holy Spirit working within him.

Andrew again quotes Cyril against himself and labors the ob-vious point that all the members of the Trinity work together; hence the Son and the Spirit might each be taken as the subject of any miracle. Theodoret takes the same line but uses a much larger battery of scriptures to prove merely that the Spirit is said to be at work in Christ's ministry. He concedes the anathema for the most part, however, so long as it is not taken to imply that the Spirit is not thereby an essentially functioning part of the god-head. For Cyril this is all utterly beside the point. Indeed, Cyril's whole burden is to prove that any miracle can be predicated of a number of individuals equally, that they belong equally to Son and Spirit. The point of the anathema, he argues, is to prevent division of Christ into two "concrete existences" (*hypostases*), and he refers back, as usual, to the more radical statements made by Nestorius in his published sermons. Even Theodoret's more cau-tious statements entail a non-unified Christ, he argues.

Cyril's aim in these treatises is to prove not merely that the anathemas are a necessary bulwark against Nestorius but also that the whole Antiochene position is wide open to Nestorian tendencies. This is what would lead Cyril in later years to turn his ire on the teachers of that tradition, on Diodore and Theo-dore.

Tenth anathema: that the fact that Christ was a "high priest" does not mean that he made offerings on his own behalf as if the "human" part of Christ needed to be atoned for.

This anathema appears to offer Theodoret a perfect oppor-tunity to expound upon a text that suits his purpose; the series of statements in Hebrews to the effect that Christ "became per-fect"[32] must refer to the humanity and *cannot* refer to the divin-ity: "This was the one who was beset by his own nature's weak-ness; he was not the almighty Word of God."[33] With rather less

---

32. Heb 5.8–9; cf. 2.10, 17–18.

33. See Theodoret's critique of the tenth anathema in *A Defense of the Twelve Anathemas against Theodoret.*

sophistication, Andrew simply asks whether, if God the Word was indeed both a high priest and himself fully God, then to which God did he offer sacrifice? Why not say both that the two elements are utterly united and at the same time that some things said in Hebrews are applicable only to one of them? Yet such a position is quite incoherent, claims Cyril, and can be no unity at all. Indeed, if you are going to talk about the "humanity" being awarded special honors quite apart from the Word (who has no need of being awarded honors), then how does he differ from any prophet or holy man? The "plan of salvation" (*oikonomia*) demands a genuine union, in which all things predicable of the man are predicable of the Word too; indeed, the two are indistinguishable after the union. However paradoxical it may seem, this is the very mystery of Christianity, and to try to squirm out of it is to deny the faith itself.

Cyril spends considerable time on this line of argument and develops a number of themes at length. Especially important is the argument against the common distinction made between "appropriate to the divinity" and "appropriate to the humanity." Once the Word had become flesh, all "human things" were made "appropriate to the divinity"; indeed, this is the very point of salvation. The Incarnation is about a self-abasement of the Word, not the glorification of a servant: "it is precisely in [the sufferings] that we can see the poverty that he willingly endured for us."[34] In the previous few sections, Cyril's task had merely been to defend the single-subject Christology against Nestorius's unguarded expressions. Now he is free to launch out on the full implications of his unitive Christology and speak of the Word as suffering, as being weak, and so forth; and hence accuse his opponents of using the word "unity" in name only.

Eleventh anathema: that the very flesh of Christ had life-giving powers; as flesh it "belonged" wholly to the Word, from whom the power to give life derives.

Theodoret zeroes in on Cyril's use of "flesh" and thinks he has uncovered a closet Apollinarianism. Andrew seems bewildered

---

34. See Cyril's defense of the tenth anathema in *A Defense of the Twelve Anathemas against Theodoret.*

at this anathema; he would be quite happy to accede to it but cannot see the point of hammering on about the flesh. He suspects that Cyril thinks Christ's flesh to be less than human (or non-human, which is tantamount to the Apollinarian position), though he does not say that here.

Cyril has dealt with this before. If to speak of the flesh implies Apollinarianism, then the evangelist was one too. He spends longer responding to Andrew's bewilderment. Citations from Nestorius, which seem to separate off the flesh of Christ from his divinity, are pitted against others from Athanasius that use expressions more conducive to Cyril's perspective.

Twelfth anathema: that God the Word actually suffered in the flesh.

Here was the most controversial of the anathemas. The previous anathema had prepared the groundwork for this one, and the theme of suffering had been covered by the tenth. The underlying problem is that of divine (im)passibility, one of the most well-trodden paths of theological debate among the eastern church traditions. The arguments presented by Theodoret and Andrew are only the opening salvoes, the first gut-reactions to these extraordinary statements that Cyril is prepared to make. How can suffering possibly be predicated of the Word without asserting that God has become passible and hence changed?

Nor is Cyril's response any more sophisticated than to say: yes, it is irrational, but that is the mystery in which we believe, and without which our salvation is meaningless. Of course, the Word suffered "not in his own nature," but Cyril cannot really explain quite what this means and why it does not imply a dissolution of his unitive Christology. Simple statements of the Christian faith should be enough, and he will end the treatise against the bishops of Oriens by quoting Gregory, Basil, and Athanasius to this end.

Summary of the principal points made by Theodoret and Andrew against Cyril's anathemas:

- To speak of the Word acting "in the flesh" implies change in the godhead.
- The lack of distinction between fleshly and divine action

implies that there has been a mixing of the natures, which is Apollinarianism.

- There is no space left in Cyril's Christology for the functioning of a human soul, the other key Apollinarian trait.
- The Scriptural descriptions of Christ are not all appropriate to the divinity, and hence Cyril's flesh-based Christology does violence to these statements.

The main points of Cyril's defense of his anathemas:

- The pointed formulae of the anathemas are needed to dismiss the extreme dualist expressions found in Nestorius's sermons and to protect the title "Mother-of-God."
- The only way to avoid the conclusion that Christ is merely the greatest prophet is to insist upon a top-down Christology that takes seriously the fact that the Word *became* flesh.
- The Christian understanding of salvation is based upon the mystery that all the human weaknesses of Christ, even death, can be predicated of the Word too.

The History of the Texts

Despite his reception in modern Western theologies, Cyril has always remained one of the towering figures of the eastern patristic tradition. Our texts thus have a rich history of manuscript transmission. They were gathered together into the dossier of documents published at the Council of Ephesus, when Cyril's anathemas became "orthodox theology." Their positive reception at Chalcedon, and the effective "canonization" of Cyril, meant that his works were always in high demand and were plumbed by both pro- and anti-Chalcedonians from the late fifth century onwards to provide "proof-texts" for their respective positions. Cyril's technique of demonstrating orthodoxy by patristic citation thus secured the future preservation of his own works among his successors.

From an early stage, independent traditions also existed in translation. The treatise *On Orthodoxy* may have been translated into Syriac within a few years of its authorship by order of Rabbula of Edessa, originally an Antiochene supporter who deserted his cause and became Cyril's key representative in the East.[35] The Syriac versions of the two *Defenses* are probably somewhat later (perhaps belonging to the final years of the fifth century), but they too circulated independently of any dossier of texts related to the council, making them a useful independent witness.[36] Latin versions of many of the texts relating to the council also exist, thanks to the indefatigable work of Marius Mercator, a serial translator and opponent of Pelagianism.

After various sixteenth-century editions of individual works, the *opera omnia* of Cyril were first collected in the seven-volume edition of Jean Aubert in 1638. These are the tomes described by Gibbon as "now peaceably slumbering by the side of their rivals."[37] Aubert's text was incorporated wholly into Migne's *Patrologia Graeca,* only to be replaced by the new editions by Philip Pusey, son of the famous Oxford tractarian. Eduard Schwartz's massive project to edit all the texts of the councils (*Acta Conciliorum Oecumenicorum* = ACO) rendered most of Pusey's work obsolete within a generation, at least for those of Cyril's works that were to be found within the major codices containing the acts of the Ephesine council.

The currently accessible editions of the Christological treatises appearing in the present volume are as follows:

On Orthodoxy to Theodosius: PG 76:1134–1200; Pusey 1877, pp. 1–153 (with Syriac version beneath); ACO 1.1.1, pp. 42–72. Note also the German translation by O. Bardenhewer, *Bibliothek der Kirchenväter,* Zweite Reihe (1935), pp. 21–78.

Defense against Theodoret: PG 76:386–452; Pusey 1875, pp. 382–497; ACO 1.1.6, pp. 107–46. Pusey's edition is printed on alternating pages with a freshly edited text of Marius Mercator's Latin, now to be found more readily at ACO 1.5, pp. 142–65.[38]

Defense against the Bishops of Oriens: PG 76:315–85; Pusey 1875,

35. King, 27–28, discusses in brief the arguments for and against Rabbula's involvement.

36. See King for further details on these Syriac versions, esp. 355–60.

37. *Decline and Fall,* vol. 4, ch. xlvii, §v.

38. Marius Mercator's Latin version of the two *Defenses* was first edited in 1673 (Garnerius).

pp. 260–381; ACO 1.1.7, pp. 33–65. Again Pusey's edition contains the Latin version, also edited at ACO 1.5, pp. 116–42.

Although Pusey did produce stilted translations of a selection of Cyril's works, none of these three treatises has appeared in modern translation before now, with the exception of Bardenhewer's German version of *On Orthodoxy* mentioned above. The modern interest in Theodoret has, however, meant that his refutations, extracted from Cyril's treatise, have twice been published in English translation, once in the series Nicene and Post-Nicene Fathers and again more recently in The Early Church Fathers series.[39]

The Present Translation and Cyril's Greek style

The present translation aims at smooth readability in modern English grammar and style. It seeks to make Cyril accessible to a wide readership and gives him a natural and easygoing manner as far as this has proved possible. Consistency of lexical renderings has only been retained for so-called "technical terms," and a list of these is provided below.

Although Cyril's style is often surprisingly informal and discursive (imitating the courtroom setting very often), it is at the same time bombastic and rhetorically high-flown. He shows off his use of Attic (often hyper-Attic) forms, although it must be noted that this characteristic was not peculiar to Cyril and in fact Theodoret is just as guilty of this tendency, which often fails to go down well among English-speaking audiences reared on a more restrained register. It is especially difficult to reproduce this in translation, and little attempt has been made really to do so, although I have often tried to give a more immediate sense of the rudeness of many of his remarks than is achieved in the rather quainter English renderings of the past.

The following are a few examples of Cyril's idiosyncratic

39. Nicene and Post-Nicene Fathers, Second Series, Vol. 3, trans. Blomfield Jackson, series eds. Philip Schaff and Henry Wace, 1892 (repr. Grand Rapids, MI: Eerdmans, 1994), 26–31; I. Pásztori-Kupán, *Theodoret of Cyrus,* The Early Church Fathers (London and New York: Routledge, 2006), 173–87.

Greek, which sought to imitate the forms of the pure classical Attic as it was taught in the schools of rhetoric:

- Atticisms such as *touti* for *touto;* *houtosi* for *houtos;* *atta* for *hatina.*
- *eiper tis* is used by Cyril far more frequently than by any other ancient author.
- He resurrects old-fashioned Homeric terms such as *tethêpoi,* which he even expands into a compound *katatethêpoi* (ACO 1.1.1, p. 51, 33), an expression totally unique to Cyril and his imitators throughout Greek literature.
- He fills his prose with rhetorical particles to make the reader feel the immediacy of a present speaker (for example, *kai men kai; kaitoi* in its combative adversative form, which is almost entirely an Attic oratorical device; *toinun,* an Attic conversational particle also typical of oratory).
- *para* as an abbreviation for *paresti.* This is a genuinely poetic Atticism, almost entirely confined to epic and tragedy and sometimes found in the linguistic conceits of the rhetoric of the second sophistic, although nobody in the post-classical age used the word as often as Cyril did.
- *ge mên* for *de* in an adversative sense, taken from Plato and Xenophon (for example, ACO 1.1.7, p. 48, 19).
- Attic hyperbaton, especially with verb placed penultimately in the clause, is very common, for example, *ho tois houtô kibdêlois nêchomenos logismois* (ACO 1.1.6, p. 125, 5).
- Fairly free use of the optative, especially in the apodosis of conditionals (for example, ACO 1.1.6, p. 124, 16; p. 125, 3).
- There are many terms and expressions that Cyril has picked up from literature and which he makes his own by frequent use. To take a single example, *athurostomia* is to be found 38 times within Cyril's corpus, out of only 55 instances in the whole of the *Thesaurus Linguae Graecae.*
- Cyril's endlessly repeated royal "we" has sometimes been turned into a singular pronoun when this seemed to produce a better result, but has as often been retained. Seeing as the bishop of Alexandria believed himself to be representing the voice of his diocese and indeed of all his predecessors, he would fain have noticed the difference.

Many words relating to theological discourse, and especially to Christology, have been translated consistently throughout:

alloiôsis	alteration
ana meros	separate(ly), on its own terms
analloiôtos	unalterable
analambanô	assume, take upon oneself
anaphurô	blend
anthrôpotês	humanity (preferred to "manhood")
[*to*] *anthrôpinon*	humanity (a synonym of the preceding term, witness *On Orthodoxy*, §31)
asugkutôs	without confusion
atreptos	without change
charaktêr	representation
chôrizô	separate
diaireô	divide
diatomê	division
diistêmi	divide
diorizô	split
empsuchos	animate
enanthrôpêsis	being-made-man
epilambanô	take upon [one's]self
henôsis	union/unity
ho ek theou logos / ho theou logos	God's Word, *or* The Word of God
hufistanai	subsist
huparchein	exist
hypostasis	concrete existence (*kath'hupostasin*, at the level of concrete existence) [see below]
idia(i) tithêmi	set apart
idikôs	individually (*idikôs kai ana meros*, a separate individual)
idiotês	property
krasis	mixture

metabolê	transformation
merizô	separate
morphê doulou	the form of a servant
oikonomia	plan of salvation, soteriology [see below]
sarkikôs	physically, materially
sarkôsis	incarnation
sarx	flesh, body, physical, material
sugkeimai	juxtapose
sugcheô	confuse
sumbasis	conjunction
sumphurô	blend
sunapheia	connection
sunaptô	connect
sundeô	bind together
sundromê	concurrence
sunodos	convergence
sunthesis	combination
suntithêmi	combine

For the well-known Greek theological term *hypostasis*, we have chosen to use the English expression *concrete existence* in order to try to unpack the meaning a little, hopefully without appearing clumsy. Although the word has often been retained in traditional English translations, modern audiences may prefer something more immediately comprehensible, even if the full implications of the term, its usage and significance within historical theology, require more than a mere translation to grasp fully. Readers will also note that I have used the modern term *christology* in a few places where it seemed an apt way for contemporary English to render expressions such as *doxa epi Christô. Pathos* is sometimes *experience,* sometimes *suffering,* or at other times just *sensation. Oikonomia* is often rendered as "the [divine] plan of salvation," and ideas to do with *oikonomia* are sometimes *soteriology.* Such expressions may at times feel rather laborious but seem greatly preferable to the now thoroughly obsolete term "divine economy."

THREE
CHRISTOLOGICAL
TREATISES

ON ORTHODOXY TO THEODOSIUS

A "Public Oration" written by Cyril, Archbishop of Alexandria, addressed to the devout Emperor Theodosius on the subject of orthodox faith in our Lord Jesus Christ

OU, CHRIST-LOVING emperors, are the very pinnacle of human glory, a status that is incomparably far and away above everything else in the world. God has laid upon you a responsibility that is both remarkable and fitting, and your earthly prerogative parallels the universal transcendence that is unique to him. Every knee bends before him,[1] whether of thrones, rulers, principalities, or authorities.[2] They submit their necks in servitude and honor him continually with fitting praises, saying that "heaven and earth are full of his glory."[3] Anyone can see in the serenity of your faces a perfectly transparent image of such manifest and incomparable importance. Because there is nothing on earth above you, you are the fountainheads of mortal honor, the root and source of all human prosperity. Whosoever submit themselves to your royal scepter are guided thereby towards a lawful, admirable, and praiseworthy life by the beneficent nods of your authority, whereas those who do not accept your yoke will quickly fall, brought low by the might that is invested in you. As soon as the royal arms strike, their armies are routed and utterly destroyed; they immediately cast aside their foolishness and beg for mercy upon their knees. Hence your warlike and battle-hardened troops are undefeated and have conquered every part of the world. You are the object of song and of tales of renown in the

1. Is 45.23.
2. Col 1.16.
3. Is 6.3.

East as in the West; neither Southerners nor even the inhabitants of the remote North ever slacken in crowning you with their joyous voices. Furthermore, it is our Lord Jesus Christ himself who is the unshakeable foundation of your godly and pure government. It is through him, as it is written, that "rulers rule and the powerful exercise justice."[4] His will is supreme, and the successful accomplishment of every good action lies within his gift. Upon those who love him he gladly bestows the very best of all that is most precious and wonderful. I take as a sufficient proof of what I have claimed all the things that have already been granted to your rule and all that we believe is yet to be granted. I shall attempt as far as I can to expound from the Holy Scriptures themselves, albeit in brief, that being renowned for godly devotion is, in fact, the unshakeable foundation of the glory of a king.

2. Many people became rulers in the land of the Jews at various times and occupied the throne of that kingdom. Some of them were profane individuals, with no interest in fearing God, who reduced the administration of justice to lawlessness. These wretched and vicious kings plunged themselves into a deep pit of godlessness and so met equally vicious ends. After all, it is a disastrous thing to fall out with God, and to insult him in any way at all is entirely beyond the pale. But then there were other rulers who valued godliness, who loyally took pains to follow his good pleasure, and so were able effortlessly to defeat their enemies and conquer their opponents. One such was Josiah, who got rid of worshipers who offered sacrifice to idols in sacred groves and high places, who outlawed every kind of witchcraft and false prophecy, and who brought devilish and deceitful revelries to an end. By acting in this way he caused his own reign to be worthy of great renown, lauded by the ancients, and a source of wonder to moderns, at least to those who know how to value what pleases the mind of God. Notwithstanding the fact that your ancestors and you yourselves have acted quite rightly in this department, I reckon it may still be appropriate to mention what wise King Hezekiah accomplished back then, for the mor-

4. Prv 8.15.

al of that story too would be of immeasurable benefit to your godly rule.

3. There was a man from Babylon in Persia named Rhapsaces who, so the story goes, conquered the whole of Judah.[5] He first overran Samaria and then fell upon Jerusalem itself with a vast army under his command. He had a phalanx of cavalry (difficult to control, equally difficult to withstand) and hoplite foot soldiers as numerous as grains of sand. Haughty beyond measure and full of barbarian arrogance, he brought siege machines and all the material of war against its walls. He promised to capture the holy city with the same force that he had used against all the other cities, and he defied them with unrepeatable insults, throwing abuse at them and giving rein to his intemperate and unbridled tongue against God. He said that, even if God did want to save them, they would be insane to trust in him for succor. When people then came and told the king all about what this perverse man with his Persian arrogance had dared to say, he was visibly pained by such godless blasphemies and thought carefully about the prophecy that the city would be captured. So he donned the appropriate garments and ascended to God's temple and there openly assuaged the divine wrath by his prayers and absolved himself of any guilt arising from these blasphemies. And the result? He once again made the Lord of Hosts well-disposed and propitious; he defeated the Assyrian, despite not being armed for battle with well-trained cavalry nor having the use of skilled marksmanship or of spearmen, and with absolutely no tactical experience. Rather, by divine decree alone, the whole Assyrian army was sent to its doom in a single night. "The angel of the Lord went out," it says, "and did away with 185,000 of the Assyrian force. And when they got up in the morning, they found all the dead bodies."[6] This is the fruit of godly religion and of taking no notice of any voice that is set against God's own glory.

5. See 2 Kgs 18–19 and Is 36–37. The old Greek translation of Kings understood the Hebrew word *Rab-Shakeh* to be the name of the Assyrian general, as also did all early modern translations. The word is in fact an Assyrian term for a military commander and is usually so translated in modern versions.

6. 2 Kgs 19.35; Is 37.36.

4. I am of the opinion that what should pass the king's pious ears ought never to be godless or blasphemous, but rather those things that render God his due and fitting praise, things that are wholly above any censure or reproof. So, seeing that I have what is best at heart, I am necessarily spurred on to put down in this book the tradition of the true and apostolic faith, by way of offering some spiritual gift to your majesty, and also to the truly God-loving Empresses, whose refulgence is second only to your own calm sereneness. One of them exults in those children of yours, for whom so many prayers were offered, and so brings to your throne the hope of permanence; the other boasts in her fruitful chastity and takes her share of the burdens of your renowned kingship.[7] Although those renowned crowns of yours are lit up by precious stones from India, nonetheless what really provides ornament to the perceptive mind and soul is an orthodox and unblemished faith. Because you hold onto this faith so boldly, I present this work as a foundation for your intelligence, a light for your soul, and a crown for your heart. For it is written, "Wisdom is better than precious stones; nothing is her equal in value."[8] So I will try to speak briefly about how the Only-Begotten was made man and what the mystery about it really is. We can try to do this as well as we may, but only so far as is permitted to those who are looking into a mirror and an enigma and whose knowledge is only partial,[9] indeed is limited by the extent of the assistance that the Spirit provides.[10] Thus Paul himself, as God's mouthpiece, writes, "No one says, Jesus is Lord, except by the Holy Spirit, and no one says, Let Jesus be anathema, except by Beelzebul."[11]

5. But it is possible that someone will retort, "Seeing as you are seeking to enter into battle with this subject and have the gall to undertake such a burdensome task, please give us a

7. These empresses were Theodosius's wife, Eudocia, and his sister, Pulcheria. The latter was considerably older than her brother and was in many ways the true power behind the throne. It was vital for Cyril to win the favor of these powerful women, and for this reason he addressed another treatise *On Orthodoxy* especially to them.

8. Prv 8.11.

9. 1 Cor 13.12.

10. Eph 4.7; Phil 1.19.

11. 1 Cor 12.3.

clear and definite Christology that is precise, honest, and cannot be gainsaid." For different people are intoxicated by different sorts of ideas and thereby disfigure the divine revelations on this subject that are found in the New and the Old Testaments. We know perfectly well there is no doctrine that these madmen have not experimented with. They fall so very readily into the "depths" of hell,[12] as it is written, and into the snare of death, "knowing neither what they are saying nor what they are making assertions about."[13] So we now have to work our way through the nonsense and pompous arguments that each of these groups has produced.

6. Some people have dared to believe and to claim that the Word of God the Father did appear as a man, but that he did not bear the flesh of the Holy Virgin, the Mother-of-God; instead, they misrepresent him as being nothing but a semblance of the mystery.[14] There are then others who allege that they would be embarrassed to appear to be worshiping a man, and so refuse to crown earthly flesh with heavenly honor. A mixture of excessive ignorance and baseless scruples leads them, in their sickness, to argue that the Word, which was begotten of God the Father, was transformed into a nature constituted of bones, nerves, and flesh. These wretched types ridicule the idea that Emmanuel was born of a virgin, and they condemn as being positively indecent the wonderful dispensation that is so proper to the divine.[15] There is another group that has believed God the Word, he who is co-eternal with the Father, to have been a latecomer and to have been called into existence only at the very moment when he was "allocated the job" of being born in the flesh.[16] There are still others who are led to such a point of ungodly insanity that they claim that the Word does not have

12. Prv 9.18.

13. 1 Tm 1.7.

14. Cyril is thinking of the Docetism of the Gnostics insofar as their doctrine was understood by the patristic tradition.

15. This is the view discussed in Athanasius's *Letter to Epictetus,* an authority and a text closely followed by Cyril throughout the Nestorian controversy.

16. "allocated the job": Cyril is using an expression from ancient Athenian politics for the allocation of ministerial tasks by lot.

his own concrete existence, but that it was a mere "verbal expression" that became a man, a sound that does not mean anything until it is actually uttered. Marcellus and Photinus were among their number.[17] It seems right to others also to believe that the Only-Begotten became a man and that he also became flesh, but that this assumed flesh was never completely endowed with a rational soul that has a mind like our own. They bind the Word of God together with the temple of the holy Virgin into a single unity, or so they aver, and then assert that the Word dwelt in this temple and that he made the assumed body his very own, himself filling the place left by the rational and thinking soul.[18] Others again proclaim quite the opposite to this last group and turn their ideas on their heads.[19] They affirm that Emmanuel is constituted and formed from God the Word together with a rational soul and a body, that is, a truly complete humanity, but that does not mean that their Christology is actually healthy or faultless, for they divide the single Christ into two, introduce a gross division between them, and so represent each one of them as having a separate existence. They maintain that one of these parts is completely human and was born of a virgin, while the other one is the Word of God the Father. They never really specify what is meant by the nature of the Word and the nature of the flesh, nor do they wish to dwell on the different expressions themselves (although on this point they do no injustice to the true doctrine, since divine and carnal natures are not identical). Yet they set the one apart as a separate and individual man, call the other one God and the genuine natural Son, and then at the same time still call themselves Christians! Here are the exact words they dared to write in composing their little pamphlets on the subject:

17. Marcellus of Ancyra, convicted of Sabellianism, taught that the Son was a "mere word," an emanation from the Father that became Logos and Son only at the Incarnation; Photinus said that the Word existed in God as does a (human) "word" in a person, whereas the "Son" did not pre-exist the Incarnation (see Epiphanius, *Panarion* 71–72).

18. Cyril always had to take great pains to distance his own position from that of Apollinarius described here.

19. Cyril ends his heresiology with a longer discussion of Nestorianism.

The one is truly and by nature the Son, the Word of God the Father, while the other is son only by homonymy. The Word of the Father (he later adds) is not flesh but took upon himself a man. For the Only-Begotten is essentially and on his own account the Son of God, who created everything; but the man which he assumed, although not God by nature, may be given the Son's name homonymously because the Son of God truly did take it onto himself. For the verse "No one knows the Son except the Father"[20] shows that the Son is truly and by nature [begotten] of the Father, whereas Gabriel's message, "Do not be afraid, Mary, for you have found favor in God's sight; and behold, you will conceive in the womb and bear a son, and you will call his name Jesus,"[21] applies rather more to the manhood.

[A. Docetism]

7. But although this is their position, it is not ours. How so? Because the arguments of the heterodox are never going to persuade those who are traveling on the straight path to switch to a road that twists and turns in the wrong direction. It would take an enormous amount of time if someone wanted to develop lengthy arguments against each of these points in turn and carry their inquiry right through to its conclusion, and this would hardly be time well spent; in fact, he would have to endure a heavy sweat while barely staying on the straight and narrow. So we must put aside any thought of disputing at great length or in much detail, and just try to launch a minor investigation against each heresy. Let us turn first of all to the Docetists and say to them, "You are mistaken, because you do not know the Scriptures," nor "the great mystery of godliness," namely, Christ, "who was manifest in the flesh, was justified in the Spirit, was seen with the angels, was proclaimed among the nations, was believed on in the world, and was raised up to glory."[22] These enemies must of necessity either propose a statement of faith that would have been shameful to our predecessors, thereby calling the teachers of the faith liars (the very ones whom Christ commanded to "go and teach all nations"),[23] or else, if they shudder at the thought of doing such a thing,

---

20. Mt 11.27.
22. Mt 22.29; 1 Tm 3.16.
21. Lk 1.30, 31.
23. Mt 28.19.

then they should elect to adopt a sound Christology, say fare-
well to their own foolishness, hold fast to the Holy Scriptures,
and set themselves upon the straight path of the saints, so as to
arrive at the actual truth.

8. This "mystery of godliness" is for us, I believe, none other
than the very Word of God the Father, who "was manifest in the
flesh."[24] He was born of the holy Virgin, the Mother-of-God, and
"took the nature of a servant."[25] He was seen by the angels who
celebrated at his birth, "Glory to God in the highest, and peace
upon earth, goodwill among men."[26] Moreover, they pointed
out to the shepherds that God the Word had come for us in
the flesh when they said, "Behold, today in the city of David a
Savior has been born to you, who is Christ the Lord. And this
shall be the sign: you shall find a baby wrapped up and lying
in a manger."[27] Given the particular circumstances of his birth
from a virgin and his physical act of becoming visible, surely it is
a useless notion, complete stuff and nonsense, to slur the wholly
transparent plan of salvation with the title of "semblance"? For
if it were nothing but a shadow and a semblance, rather than a
genuine incarnation, and if the Virgin did not really give birth,
then the Word of God the Father did not take upon himself the
seed of Abraham, and neither has he become like his brothers.[28] For our own situation is nothing like a shadow or a "semblance." Rather, we dwell in tangible and visible bodies, and so,
because we are clothed in this earthly body, we are susceptible
to physical sensation and decay.

9. So unless the Word became flesh, he would not "be able to
help those who are being tempted because he himself suffered
and was tempted."[29] A shadow cannot feel pain. The fact of his
being "with us" would mean nothing at all. That back of his that
he offered on our behalf—what sort of back was it?[30] That cheek
that he exposed to his assailants and which endured lashes from
the Jews—what sort of cheek was it?[31] Those nails that were driv-

---

24. 1 Tm 3.16.   25. Phil 2.7.
26. Lk 2.14.   27. Lk 2.11, 12.
28. Heb 2.16, 17.   29. Heb 2.18.
30. Is 50.6.   31. Ibid.

en through his hands and feet, how can we possibly think of this as happening to one whose appearance was not really physical? That side of his that Pilate's soldiers pierced and from which those who were watching saw his precious blood flowing out with water—what sort of side was it?[32] If I have to go on like this, then Christ neither died for us nor was he raised again. Were we to allow this viewpoint, our faith would have become empty; the cross, which is the salvation and life of the world, would have vanished; and all hope for those who have fallen asleep in the faith utterly destroyed. The blessed Paul saw it this way as well. He said, "Above all I have passed on to you what I also received, that Christ died for our sins according to the Scriptures, that he was buried, that he rose on the third day, according to the Scriptures, and that Cephas, and then the twelve, saw him; later more than five hundred brothers at once saw him, of whom the majority are even now alive, although some have fallen asleep; then James saw him; then all the apostles; last of all, as if an afterbirth, even I saw him."[33] And again, a little further on, "If it is preached that Christ has been raised from the dead, how can some of you say that there is no resurrection of the dead? If there is no resurrection of the dead, Christ has not been raised; if Christ has not been raised, our preaching is empty, and empty also is our faith. We will be found to be false witnesses of God, because we have witnessed about God, that he raised Christ, whom he did not raise—if indeed the dead are not raised."[34] Tell me, then, how does a shadow die? How could the Father have raised up Christ if he were a shadow and a "semblance" and as such could not be bound by death's snares? Get rid of their vomit! Let us reckon their opinions as naught but fables and the dregs of an unholy mind. These are just the sort of people that our Savior's disciple was warning us against when he wrote, "for many false prophets have gone out into the world. This is how you recognize the Spirit of God: every spirit that confesses that Jesus Christ has come in the flesh is from God; every spirit that does not confess Jesus is not from God. This is what you heard about the

32. Jn 19.34.
33. 1 Cor 15.3–8.
34. 1 Cor 15.12–15.

Antichrist, that he is coming and is now already in the world."[35] You see, if he did not become a man, then he has also not ascended in the flesh to his God and Father in heaven, nor will he return to us from heaven, namely, physically, as a man.

[B. Theomorphism]

10. Then there is the opinion held by others out of their infinite stupidity, that the Word that was begotten of God declined to be born by means of the holy Virgin, thereby holding human nature in contempt, but that instead he was transformed into earthly flesh. These folk are blaspheming against God's way of salvation and like to find fault with his plans. For the Word, who is the Creator of all and rich in mercy, emptied himself for us and became a man,[36] "born of a woman,"[37] so that, "since the children are partakers of flesh and blood"—that is, we are—"so he also likewise might partake of the same things so that, by death, he might defeat the one who holds the power of death, that is, the devil, and release those who were held in slavery all their lives by their fear of death."[38] That is what Holy Scripture says. They are thereby claiming that his totally perfect and wonderful plan is unworthy of him, as if their own ideas were some sort of improvement, and they find fault with his wise plans. They say that we should not accuse the Only-Begotten of having been involved with a woman's labor pains.[39] Instead (they say) we ought to think that the Word's nature was transformed into a rotten and earth-born body, and they imagine some transformation in the one who knows no change. The divine nature is firmly fixed in its own virtues, and its essential inner permanence is unshakeable. A nature that is created and that has come to exist within time might indeed experience alteration, and this fact is perfectly in line with appropriate and valid argu-

---

35. 1 Jn 4.1–3.   36. Phil 2.7.
37. Gal 4.4.   38. Heb 2.14, 15.

39. Clem. Alex., *Strom.* 7.16, describes the debate over whether Mary truly experienced labor. Clement himself took the more "gnostic" position that she did not (that is, virginity remained *post partum*); theologians fighting gnostic ideas would tend to the opposite view, as, e.g., Tertullian, and Cyril here.

ments, since anything whose lot it is to have a beginning to its existence is necessarily changeable in virtue of what is already sown within it. But God, who is beyond all intellect, generation, and corruption, has an existence that completely transcends all notion of change. And just as by the logic of his own nature he stands above and beyond everything that has been called into being, and that to an unparalleled degree, so he also stands over and above the things that normally happen to such created beings. He has no knowledge or experience of things that harm. So the Godhead exists in unchangeable perfection, while created things constantly experience flux and change. The prophet Jeremiah was well aware of this and, seeing as he was a good philosopher, declared of God, "You dwell forever while we perish forever,"[40] since the Godhead sits upon his own throne, ever ruling and governing the universe without being subject to any sensation, while we, having as we do natures that are so readily altered and altogether prone to changing, "perish forever"; that is, we are at any and every moment subject to decay and change. Indeed, no external accidents ever cause the Godhead to undergo even the slightest transformation to his own permanence. Furthermore, a nature that decays and changes, that is, one that has been created, may never be enriched by an inherent resistance to change, nor may a creature ever boast in the virtues of the divine nature as if they were its own. If it tried to, it would deserve to be told, "What do you have that you have not received?"[41] The fact that the nature of the Word is altogether unalterable and unchangeable, while all that comes to be is changeable, was the subject of an especially apt lament made by the psalmist in the spirit of the blessed David: "The heavens are destroyed, but you remain; all things wear out like a garment, and like a piece of clothing you discard them, and they are thrown out; but you are the same and your years know no end."[42] How can it possibly be that the Word of God remained ever the same if it is also true to say that he gave up being wholly immoveable and descended into something that at one time

40. Bar 3.3.   41. 1 Cor 4.7.
42. Ps 102.26–27 (101.27–28 LXX).

did not exist, that he was transformed into a physical nature, something that was born to die? Surely any such suggestion is total madness. There can be no doubt about it.

1 1. It is time now to set against those people's foolish ideas something yet more foolish, for surely it is just as likely that an earthly body might someday gain the power to rise up to the divine nature and acquire the constitution of that Being that is above everything. After all, if the divine nature can itself be turned into a physical one, which is what those abovementioned idiots suggested, then why should there be any reason for a body not to rise above its own lowly nature and remold itself into the Divinity, into the Highest Being? But for us, we prefer to follow the Holy Scriptures than to oblige their lunacy with any credence. The prophet says, "Behold, the Virgin will conceive and bear a son, and they will give him the name Emmanuel,"[43] and because this prophecy was then authenticated by blessed Gabriel when he explained the heavenly decree to the Virgin by saying, "Do not be afraid, Mary, for behold, you shall conceive and bear a son, and you shall call his name Jesus,"[44] we therefore believe that Emmanuel truly was born of a woman and do not thereby reject the magnificent honor that belongs to the human nature. This is orthodox doctrine, for it was not his own nature that the Only-Begotten took hold of (for this would not have benefited our condition at all), nor was it an angelic nature, but, as the Scripture says, it was "the seed of Abraham."[45] For it was thus, and not in any other way, that the race that had fallen into decay could be saved.

[C. Arianism]

1 2. What! Is there not something else that should cause us to be shocked?[46] There are some who have all but taken their leave

---

43. Is 7.14.   44. Lk 1.30, 31.
45. Heb 2.16.

46. There is some uncertainty about this chapter. Does it belong with the discussion of Theomorphism in the previous chapters, or does Chapter Twelve appear to be part of the refutation of Theomorphism? It speaks of a doctrine of the Son coming into being at the Incarnation, a belief usually associated with

of the inspired Scriptures and are giving up their own minds to the spirits of error, who have fallen into misguided ideas and puerile idiocies because they reckon that the Creator of the ages, God the Word, who is co-eternal with God the Father, must have begun his existence only at that moment when the flesh actually came into being, that the one who is beyond all eternity and time made his appearance only as a late-comer, that it is only in more recent history, at the time of the Incarnation, that God became a Father, and that it was only then that he interjected, so to speak, by means of that temple born of the Virgin,[47] the very one through whom and in whom are all things, into a state of being and having his own concrete existence. Surely these folk have charged right up to the very peak of evil when they give rein to such a silly, execrable fiction[48] and fill their minds with pure stupidity? Truly "their throats are an open grave; they deceive with their tongues; the poison of snakes is under their lips; and their mouths are full of cursing and bitterness."[49] Yet the one through whom all things came to be must surely also have existed before all things. What can they possibly do with this citation from John? "In the beginning was the Word, and the Word was with God, and the Word was God; he existed in the beginning with God; all things came about through him, and apart from him nothing came about that did come about,"[50] and also, "the one who was from the beginning, whom we heard, whom we caught sight of with our eyes, whom we saw, whom our hands touched, concerning the Word of Life—and this life appeared, and we saw and witnessed it, and proclaimed to you the eternal life, which was with the Father and which appeared among us."[51] Christ himself indicated to the Jews that

Marcellus and Photinus, the subjects of the next section. According to Hilary, *De Trin.* 10.50–51, however, the two beliefs formed some sort of continuum, and Cyril does not separate them too radically.

47. "temple": theologians of Cyril's day frequently use the term "the temple" to refer to the physical manifestation of the Logos on earth. Although it is not a term used by modern theologians, it will be found throughout these treatises.

48. 1 Tm 4.7.

49. Rom 3.13, 14 (but quoted from the Septuagint version of Ps 13.3).

50. Jn 1.1–3.

51. 1 Jn 1.1–3.

his own existence extended back into the mists of time, since when they exclaimed, "You are not yet fifty years old, yet you have seen Abraham!" the reply they got back was, "Truly I tell you, before Abraham was, I am."[52] Here we have something about whom we can say both "he was" and "I am" without adding any predicates—who can possibly perceive a moment when such a one first came into existence? How could he who has existed above all intellect from the beginning allow himself to be brought into existence at a particular time? If anyone wanted to take up these questions at leisure, it would be quite straightforward to deploy texts from the inspired Scriptures that would do great damage to these hare-brained ideas of theirs. It is barely worth bothering about what is so plainly unsound and so easily refuted. So let us turn now instead to a doctrine that is of a type with those we have already convicted.

[D. Marcellianism]

13. Some people falsify the beauty of the truth, as if they were minting false coin, "exalting their horn to the heavens and speaking unrighteousness against God,"[53] as the Scripture says. They imagine that the Only-Begotten did not have real being or subsist as an individual, that he did not have his own concrete existence. The wretches suggest that he is but a sound, merely a "word" pronounced by God which makes its dwelling in a man; they imply that Jesus, notwithstanding that he is holier than all the saints, is still not actually God. It is just as our Savior's disciple asked, "Who is the liar, if not he who denies that Jesus is the Christ? This man is the antichrist, who denies the Father and the Son. Whoever denies the Son has not the Father, but the one who confesses the Son has the Father also."[54] They are both recognized through each other, and each in the other, and that both for humans and the holy angels. Nobody can inquire as to what a father is unless he presupposes mentally a son who subsists and is begotten; and vice versa, nobody can inquire into what a son may be unless he clearly realizes that there is a fa-

52. Jn 8.57.   53. Ps 75.5 (74.6 LXX).
54. 1 Jn 2.22–23.

ther who begets. I would argue that we must surely say that, if the Son is unreal, then it follows of necessity that neither can one truly think of the Father as a father. Where is the father who has not actually had a child? Similarly, if the child he begot neither subsisted nor existed at all, then the child would not be anything, since for something not to subsist is in fact not to be at all; it amounts to total non-being. The consequence would be that God is the Father of non-being.

14. Well then, my dear friends, if I had a chance to talk to these interpreters, I would tell them, "Your ideas are so much pointless nonsense; if that is not the case, then answer me this question: how is the love that God the Father has for us anything extraordinary? If he gave the Son for us, the one that according to you has no separate existence, then he has given us a non-being; neither has the Word become flesh, nor suffered the precious cross, nor rendered death impotent, nor risen to life again. If, as you have it, he is non-being and unreal, how can any of these things be? The message of Holy Scripture has deceived the faithful, and the assurance of faith has come to naught. What then? Does the holy word not indicate to us that the Son exists in the form of God, and does it not say that he is the image and representation of the one who has begotten him?[55] Everyone surely, at the very least, agrees that images are like their archetypes; it could not possibly be otherwise. If, then, the image does not have its own concrete existence, or the representation is thought not to exist on its own account, then one must admit from force of logic that the one from whom the character derives is also without concrete existence, and the dishonor of the image redounds completely upon the archetype.

15. Tell me whether Philip, that keen disciple of Christ, when he asked, "Lord, show us the Father, and that will be enough for us,"[56] expected to see a Father who is and who subsists or one who is neither? I think there is no doubt that the answer would have to be the former. If the Son is a non-being without subsistence, as the unbridled effrontery of those people suggests, why

55. Phil 2.6; Heb 1.3.
56. Jn 14.8.

would he present himself to us as the image and exact representation of the Father, when he said, "I have been with you such a long time, Philip, and yet you do not know me? Whoever has seen me has seen the Father. Do you not believe that I am in the Father and the Father is in me? I and the Father are one"?[57] I do not reckon that one can discern something that subsists within something that does not, nor can anyone believe that what is could be the same as what is not. If so, then how could the Father be "in the Son," or the Son "in the Father"? Are we not driven to the conclusion that, if the Word does not exist on his own account, then the Father is himself in danger because he would have a non-being within himself and would himself be thought of as existing within a non-being? In short, whatever does not completely and properly exist can only be considered as a non-being. This argument is very uneven (and suffers enormously from incoherence), but nonetheless this dogma of our opponents does result in these incongruities. It would not be unreasonable to be rather surprised to learn that the Father managed to create what exists by means of a Son who does not. Again, if you were to ask whether it is better to exist or not, surely you would say straight off that the former is better. The one who grants being to things that once did not exist is considered good, and the Creator. This is how things should naturally be. Hence the creature must be better off than the one through whom all things were brought into being, since the latter is said not to subsist, while the others do subsist and are thought of as having existence. What utter tripe! Get rid of such blasphemy! As it is written, "The Word of God is living and active."[58] He also says, "I am the life,"[59] yet if he does not subsist, how could he be reckoned as "life"? No, he is Life by his very nature, and he never lies. To deny that the Word begotten of God subsists is a rotten lie, the dregs of a witless mind. He said himself to Moses, "I am the one that is."[60] How could anyone think for a moment that the one who truly is is not secure in his own concrete existence? Therefore, we can reasonably write off those who put forward such arguments as the most ignorant of all.

57. Jn 14.9–10.
59. Jn 14.6.
58. Heb 4.12.
60. Ex 3.14.

[E. Apollinarianism]

16. Those of us who have been taught how to search out the truth equally do not approve of those who argue that the flesh which was united to the Word was devoid of a rational soul. They introduce into the universe a Word clothed with flesh that is accorded only living and sensile motion, while they attribute the activity of mind and soul to the Only-Begotten. They fear—I know not why—to confess that the Word is united by nature to human flesh endowed with a rational soul. They seem to think that the tradition of our ancient faith has no firm grounding, and instead reckon they ought to follow their own desires and all-too-human arguments. Their ignorant opinions are truly "contrary to what one ought to think."[61] And what are the grounds of their position? Let me explain. From our position, we say that the "mediator between God and men,"[62] as the Scripture expresses it, is composed of a manhood that is like our own, complete according to its proper definition, and the Son, that is, the Only-Begotten, who is by nature manifested from the Father. We maintain that a convergence occurred, an indescribable concurrence that brought about a unity between otherwise unequal and dissimilar natures, although we recognize a single Christ, Lord, and Son, at the same time both God and man, both in reality and conceptually. We continue to hold that this unity is wholly unbreakable, since we believe that the Only-Begotten and the firstborn are the same individual, the Only-Begotten insofar as he is the Word of God the Father who appeared from his very essence, and firstborn insofar as he became a man and was one "among many brothers."[63] "Just as there is one God the Father, from whom are all things, so also there is one Lord Jesus Christ, through whom are all things."[64] For we recognize that the Word, through whom all things exist, is God by nature, even when he became flesh, that is to say, a man.

17. At no point, however, do their theories on this subject match our own. You see, although even they concede that there

---

61. Rom 12.3.   62. 1 Tm 2.5.
63. Rom 8.29.   64. 1 Cor 8.6.

is a single Jesus Christ and reject any division of Emmanuel
into two as being a wholly profane thing to do, they continue
nonetheless to claim that the Word of God has been united to
a flesh that is stripped of any human, rational soul. There is,
they reckon, a plausible argument to prove this. They argue
that what converged and combined into a single complete entity were parts, and incomplete parts at that, seeing as an existent
that is complete on its own account or in its own nature should
not have to be [constituted as] a combination of [incomplete]
parts.[65] They go on therefore to argue that one should avoid saying that the temple that was united to the Word was [already] a
complete man, so as to preserve the genuine and absolute nature of the combination that we think of as applying to Christ.
And they would, I think, add the following argument as well: if
Emmanuel is composed of a perfect man and the Word who is
from the Father, then there is a significant risk attached, and in
fact this may necessarily entail conceiving and speaking of two
Sons, and even of two Christs, even if that is not our intention.
How can we respond [to this argument]? Firstly, it is not appropriate to offend by pedantic quibbling the ancient tradition
of the faith that was passed down to us from the holy apostles
themselves,[66] nor to subject what lies beyond the intellect to a
detailed investigation, nor to barge into the middle of a debate
and rashly make judgments such as, "This argument is the right
one, while that is the wrong one." It were better by far to leave
the path of our own considerations in the hands of God, who
is all-wise, rather than profanely to critique what he has sanc-
tioned. For we shall take heed of what [the Scripture] clearly
says, "My counsels are not like your counsels, nor are your ways
like my ways, but as far as the heaven is from the earth, so far is
my way from your ways and your thoughts from my thoughts."[67]

65. Combination (*sunthesis*) refers to the Aristotelian theory of mixtures set
out in *De generatione et corruptione* 1.10 and elsewhere; although Aristotle himself
used the term *sunthesis* technically to mean a composition of elements that is
only a spatial juxtaposition, he elsewhere uses the term loosely of any one of the
various kinds of combinations that he distinguishes.

66. Reading *katalupein,* a distinctively Cyrilline expression, for *kataluein.*

67. Is 55.8.

18.[68] We shall never worship two sons, nor speak of two Christs, despite the fact that we believe that the temple which has been united to the Word is endowed with a rational soul.[69] Even if, following what they see as the right line of argument, even if they were to say [that the union is made up] separately of the flesh and the Word that comes from God the Father, they would not be compelled thereby to confess a duality of Christs on account of having separated out the flesh and the Only-Begotten;[70] so in just the same way we also say that "the Word of God adapted himself and was united, in a way that can be neither expressed nor conceived, with a complete humanity like our own, in accordance with the logic of his own nature," without thereby thinking of this as a duality of sons; instead, [we think of him as] one and the same individual, being as he is God by nature, issuing from the very substance of God the Father, who in these last stages of history became a man, who was born

68. A chapter is probably missing here. In the parallel text, *De Incarnatione*, Cyril adds a further answer to his rhetorical question in ch. 17: "Then, what wise men have found to be reasonable in these matters is found in fact to be wholly useless and foolish, for if one opts to strip that divine temple of a rational soul, then a convergence will in no way come about from two incomplete [parts]. It is generally accepted that in the case of a whole person, i.e., body and soul, the soul on its own is only a part. But in the case of God the Word, my friends, this cannot be thought of as a part of something, nor as being incomplete, since he is perfect in his own nature. Where, then, is the convergence into a single complete being from two incomplete parts, if [it results] from the Word that is complete and the flesh that is not, insofar as this is what leads to the definition of a whole man who is complete in accordance with his own nature?" It may well be that the passage in question was deemed to yield too much to the Apollinarian argument and so was dropped by Cyril when he rewrote the *De Incarnatione* into the *De Recta Fide ad Theodosium*. On the other hand, the Armenian translation has the missing passage, and there is an obvious gap in the sense without it. See G.-M. de Durand, ed., *Deux dialogues christologiques*, Sources chrétiennes 97 (Paris: Éditions du Cerf, 1964), 520–21.

69. *De Incarnatione* has this: "despite the fact that we believe that the convergence of Emmanuel into a unity was brought about from a perfect man and God the Word."

70. *De Incarnatione* adds, "They accept Emmanuel as the one Lord Jesus Christ—and in this they perceive to think aright." This may be another case of Cyril's sensitiveness to the accusation of Apollinarianism, which was being cast in his direction at the time of writing.

through the holy Virgin, Mother-of-God, and whom we and the holy angels worship in accordance with the Scriptures.

19. And suppose they say that all we need [suggest] is that the Only-Begotten paid us a visit and that because he wanted to be visible to those on earth, to live among men,[71] and to show us the way of the gospel kingdom, he wrapped himself, for the purposes of the divine plan of salvation, in a flesh like our own (after all, the divine is invisible in its own nature). If they so argue, they will be exposed as ignorant of the overall purpose[72] of the Incarnation and wholly failing to understand "the great mystery of religion."[73] If the Incarnation of the Only-Begotten (that is, his "being-made-man") had no occasion besides making himself visible to those on earth, then nothing at all was added to human nature, and it would make far more sense for us to adhere to the opinions of the Docetists! They are the wretches who clothe the Word in flesh and an earthly body and tell tall tales about how he became visible as a man on earth. Yet they are easily exposed as having totally missed the truth. If, despite his becoming flesh, the Word of God brought no benefit to human nature, then why not just say that he was entirely free from physical impurity and therefore seemed to be making use of an earthly body to achieve his stated purpose? Then what was the reason for his visit? How did he become man? Why did he do it? We can provide the answers for anyone who cares to ask such questions; in fact, the Holy Scripture will do the teaching. Come, my friend, to where the holy words may be found, apply your mind's eye carefully to what the holy apostles said, and you will see clearly what you seek. This is what Paul the wise, in whom "Christ himself was speaking,"[74] said for us: "Since the

71. Bar 3.38.

72. Purpose: *skopos,* a key technical term for Cyril in his understanding of the Bible. Cyril means that the whole phenomenon of incarnation had a goal and an objective that pervades every aspect of it and that is the interpretive key for understanding every part of it. See J. David Cassel, "Key Principles in Cyril of Alexandria's Exegesis," *Studia patristica* 37, ed. M. F. Wiles and E. J. Yarnold with P. M. Parvis (Leuven: Peeters, 2001): 413–15.

73. 1 Tm 3.16.

74. 2 Cor 13.3.

children have partaken of flesh and blood, so he likewise also shared in the same, so that through death, he might destroy the one who has power over death, that is, the devil, and set free those who, because they feared death, were held in slavery all their lives."[75] He also gave us another explanation: "That which was impossible for the law in that it was weakened through the flesh, God [did], sending his own Son in the likeness of sinful flesh, and on behalf of sin, [and] condemned sin in the flesh, so that the righteous things of the law might be fulfilled in us, who walk not by flesh but by spirit."[76]

20. After all, is it not totally obvious to absolutely everyone that the Only-Begotten came among us as a complete man in order to set our earthly bodies free from the decay that is foreign to it, and that the saving union was the means by which he injected himself into our own way of life? And also so that by making the human soul his very own he might demonstrate that it was superior to sin, as if he had dyed it like a piece of wool with his own nature's unshakeable immutability? I believe that we need analogies like this when we discuss matters that are so hard to understand; for I am looking at these divine mysteries, which are way over my head, "as if in a mirror and as an enigma."[77] In fact I think that this [analogy] is especially apposite, since it contains a picture, or rather an accurate parallel. Just as the flesh overcame the power of death and decay because it became the Word's own [flesh], he who gives life to all things, so I would argue that the soul similarly, since it belonged to him who knows no fault, was rooted in its unalterable condition with respect to virtue and remained incomparably stronger than that tyrant sin that has been around us for so long. Christ was the first and only man upon earth "who did not sin and in whose mouth no deceit was found."[78] He was established as the root and the first-fruits of those who are being transformed into the newness of life in the Spirit. By his grace and through participation [with him], he will bring physical incorruptibility and the absolute security of divinity to the entire human race. Because

75. Heb 2.14, 15.
77. 1 Cor 13.12.
76. Rom 8.3, 4.
78. 1 Pt 2.22.

he knew this, Paul, God's mouthpiece, wrote, "Just as we bear the image of the earthly man, so we shall bear the image of the heavenly man."[79] The expression "the image of the earthly man" indicates the tendency to sin and the death that has invaded us as a result. But "the image of the heavenly man," that is, Christ, is the certainty of sanctification, the doing-away of death and decay, and the bringing-in of incorruptibility and of life.

21. It was one complete thing with another, the complete Word of God united with a complete manhood like our own—this is what we affirm. There is no conceivable reason why he would favor the better part of us, namely, the soul, while bestowing the experiences of his living among us only upon the body. The mystery of salvation was accomplished on both levels. He made use of his own body, like an instrument, for carrying out bodily activities and its physical infirmities, at least such only as are not immoral, while his own soul experienced what is peculiarly human but not open to condemnation. We are told that he suffered hunger, that he bore with the trials of extensive travel, that he experienced violence and fear, grief and agony, and even death on the cross. He laid down his own soul for us of his own accord, without anyone forcing him to do so, "so that he might be Lord both of the dead and of the living."[80] He paid with his own flesh for the flesh of all, a gift truly sufficient, and he made his soul a redemption for the souls of all.[81] And if he took up his life again, that is because, as God, he is life by nature. Hence Peter, God's mouthpiece, said, "My brothers, I am able to speak with you openly about our great ancestor David, that he died and was buried, and that his tomb is with us even until now. But being a prophet, he knew God had sworn to him with an oath to place someone upon his throne who came from his own family, and in so saying he was speaking with foresight about Christ's resurrection, that his soul would not be abandoned to Hades, nor his body to decay."[82] It would never be ap-

79. 1 Cor 15.49.
80. Rom 14.9.
81. A key anti-Apollinarian argument that may be found in, e.g., ps-Athanasius, *Contra Apollinarem* 1.17 (PG 26:1125).
82. Acts 2.29–31.

propriate to say that the body, once it had been united to the Word, could be overcome by decay or that the divine soul was held fast at Hades' gates since, as Saint Peter said, he was not abandoned to Hades. We would not say that a nature which the mind cannot comprehend and which death cannot capture, namely, the divinity of the Only-Begotten, was escorted back up from the caverns beneath the earth. There is nothing shocking about the Word from God not remaining in Hades since he fills all things and lives among all by the energy and nature of his divinity in a manner that can hardly be described. Divinity cannot be located or enclosed or in any way measured, nor contained in any way at all.

22. What is so paradoxical and universally astonishing is that a body that is naturally corruptible should rise again (for it belonged to the incorruptible Word), while a [human] soul, after being allotted the task of joining with the Word in a unity, descended into Hades and also, by making use of a power and authority that is proper to God, showed himself to the spirits there. Furthermore, he also said, "to those in chains, 'Come out,' and to those in the darkness, 'Be free.'"[83] It seems to me that God's mouthpiece Peter was also saying something like this regarding God the Word and the soul that became his own for the sake of the saving union, "for it is better, if it is the will of God, to suffer for doing good rather than for doing evil; after all, Christ also died once for sins, the just for the unjust, that he might bring you to God, being killed as regards the body, but made alive as regards the spirit, in which," he says, "he went and preached to the spirits in prison, those who rebelled long ago."[84] I do not believe one ought to say that it was the Only-Begotten's divinity, stripped down and on its own, who descended into Hades and preached to the spirits there, since it is totally invisible (divinity is superior to what may be seen); but I will also insist that [the divine nature] did not merely "seem" or "appear" to transform itself into the form of a soul (this notion of "semblance" is to be totally rejected). But just as he himself had a physical state at

83. Is 49.9.
84. 1 Pt 3.17–20.

the time when he was living among physical people, so when he preached to the souls in Hades he had his own garment, his soul that had been united to him.

23. The way the Incarnation works is profound and cannot be expressed or even grasped by our minds, though that does not mean it is inappropriate to analyze it. Meddling in matters that do not concern us is not without its risks, and it is quite unacceptable to exceed the limits of our own intellects in our questioning and to try to think the unthinkable. Surely you appreciate that this profound mystery, which is far beyond the capabilities of the human mind, ought to be respected with an unquestioning faith. We shall safely leave for Nicodemus and others like him the insane question, "How can these things be?"[85] while unhesitatingly accepting that through which the divine Spirit has been pronounced. We shall put our trust in Christ, who says, "Truly I tell you, we speak of what we know, and we testify to what we have seen."[86] Let us leave every crazy idea, made-up story, and false opinion, and the delusion of subtle words far behind; let us put aside anything that is likely to be harmful, even if our opponents launch well-honed and pointed arguments in our direction. For our divine mystery "is not by persuasion, using clever words, but in the manifestation of the Spirit."[87]

24. So the Only-Begotten, he who is God and Lord of all just as the Scriptures say,[88] has appeared to us. When he became a man he was seen upon the earth[89] and shone upon those in the darkness, but this did not happen simply as an "appearance" (heaven forbid! for it is madness to say and think such a thing), nor did he come close to his body by changing or transforming himself in some manner (for the Word of God exists immutably, remaining always and ever the same), nor was his general existence contemporaneous with the physical existence of his body (for he is the Creator of the ages), nor did he enter a man merely as a "word" without concrete existence or as a simple

85. Jn 3.9.   86. Jn 3.11.
87. 1 Cor 2.4.   88. Ps 118.27 (117.27 LXX).
89. Bar 3.38.

verbal expression. For the one who called into existence what was not and who gave things their beginning must necessarily be pre-existent. For he is the life that issued from the life that is God the Father. Both in reality and in our minds he has his own concrete existence. But he was not wrapped with flesh alone, devoid of a rational soul. No, he was truly born of a woman, and appeared as a man, God the Word, the living one, existing and co-eternal with God the Father. He took the form of a servant, and just as he is complete in his divinity, so he is complete in his humanity. It is not a case of the single Christ, Lord, and Son merely being a juxtaposition of divinity and some flesh, but rather he is paradoxically bound together out of two complete elements, namely, humanity and divinity, into a single individual being.

[F. Dyophysitism]

25. Someone will probably ask at this point, "To whom did the holy Virgin give birth? Was it to a man or to the Word of God?" We reply: that question is wholly misguided; it is in default of what is right and true. As far as I am concerned, you ought not to allow any division after the union, nor may you reshape Emmanuel into two persons by splitting him up individually into a man and God the Word. No one should accuse us of having taken an unorthodox position here since this is just what is expressly condemned by Holy Scripture. As one of Christ's disciples said, "But you, beloved, remember the words foretold by the apostles of our Lord Jesus Christ, that they said to you, that in the last days mockers will come with their mocking, people who live in accordance with their own irreverent desires. These are those who, being sensual rather than spiritual, make divisions."[90] So there is no way there can be any division, especially if it involves talking of "two" after the union or thinking of each separately. It is appropriate for one's mind to sense a distinction between the natures (after all, human and divine natures are not identical), but at the same time as this acknowledgment, the mind

90. Jude 17–19.

must also accept the concurrence of the two into a unity. So, it was as God that he issued from God the Father, and as man that he issued from the Virgin. The Word who shone out from God the Father, in a manner that can be neither described nor imagined, is said to have also been born of a woman, descending into humanity and entering into what was not his own, not with the aim of remaining thus emptied, but rather so that he might be believed to be God and appear on earth in human form, not just as if he were dwelling inside someone but by himself becoming a man by nature while simultaneously preserving his own glory. So God's mouthpiece Paul combines these two things into a unity, namely, the divinity and the humanity, which would otherwise be so far from being consubstantial with each other and which are so utterly distinct, and he makes this combination in the context of salvation-history, and then he demonstrates that there is one single Christ out of the two elements, one Son, one God: "Paul, a servant of Christ Jesus, called out as an apostle, set apart for the Gospel of God, the Gospel which was announced beforehand through his prophets in the Holy Scriptures, which concerns his Son, the one made from the seed of David according to the flesh, and established as Son of God in power according to the Spirit of holiness."[91] Note carefully that he says that he himself was set apart for the Gospel of God and writes openly that "we do not preach ourselves, but Jesus Christ,"[92] and again, "for I decided to know nothing among you except Jesus Christ, and him crucified."[93]

26. After first calling him Son of God, he goes on to say that he was born of the seed of David and to affirm that he was "established as the Son of God." So, then, tell me how is it that one who comes from David's seed can be God? How could the Son, who is before all ages and co-eternal, insofar as he issued from God, be "established" as the Son of God, as if there were some beginning to his existing? After all, he said about himself, "The Lord said to me, 'You are my son, today I have begotten you,'"[94] where the word "today" indicates, as always, not the past but the

---

91. Rom 1.1–4.   92. 2 Cor 4.5.
93. 1 Cor 2.2.   94. Ps 2.7.

present. This mystery is surely profound, but those who separate out the parts and divide them up cannot manage it at all,
whereas for those who bind Emmanuel together into a unity,
the pure knowledge of the holy doctrines is readily comprehensible. The Son, who is co-eternal with the one from whom he
issued and who exists prior to every age, descended into human
nature, taking up humanity to himself rather than slipping away
from being God, and hence he may legitimately be thought of
as being born of David's seed and of experiencing a wholly new
human birth. What he took up into himself was not foreign to
him, but is truly his very own. It is therefore to be reckoned as
being one with him, just as one might naturally think of how
a person is constituted, a person whose nature is woven from
unlike parts, namely, soul and body, but the combined person
is still reckoned as a single individual. One sometimes names
an entire animal on the basis of just its physical body, but at
other times the combined being is meant when the soul is explicitly mentioned. We ought to accept just the same way of
talking about Christ, for there is only one Son and one Lord
Jesus Christ both before his taking flesh and when he appeared
as a man.

27. No, we shall never deny our Master and Redeemer, even
when people make a point of his human aspects and the lim-
itation that came with his self-emptying. You see, our Lord Jesus Christ spoke to the Jews as follows: "If you were children of
Abraham, you would do what Abraham did. But now you are
seeking to kill me, a man who has told you the truth—Abraham
did not do this."[95] Paul talks about this as well: "He [Jesus], in
the days of his flesh, offered up prayers and supplications to
the one who had the power to save him from death, with great
cries and tears, and he was heard because of his reverence, and
although he was a Son, he learned obedience from what he suffered."[96] Do we argue from this that Christ is to be reckoned a
mere man who is in no way superior to our own nature? Heaven
forbid! Do we allow the possibility that God's wisdom and power

95. Jn 8.39–40.
96. Heb 5.7–8.

might have come down to such a level of weakness that he was actually afraid of dying and prayed to the Father for his own salvation? Do we deprive the Emmanuel of being life by nature? Should we not rather, when we think of how descriptions of his humanity and the limitations of having a nature like ours might seem contemptible, do something truly praiseworthy by giving proper recognition to the supra-mundane glory that belongs to him by virtue of his being God, while also realizing that he is at once both man and God, or rather the God-made-man? Paul, who is so reliable for us, got right to the point when he made the following declaration: "We speak wisdom among the perfect, but not the wisdom of this age, nor of the rulers of this age, who are coming to their end, but we speak the wisdom of God, which is hidden in mystery and which none of the rulers of this age knew. If they had known, they would not have crucified the Lord of glory."[97] And then furthermore, that "the one who, being the reflection of the glory [of God] and the representation of his being, bearing all things by his powerful word, and after making purification for our sins, sat down at the right hand of the Majesty in the highest places, becoming as superior to the angels as the name that he has inherited is greater than theirs."[98] So does not being the "Lord of Glory," and being given that name, imply something far above and beyond everything in the created order that is subject to the processes of becoming? Leaving aside humanity for now (for that is a status of so little consequence), I will say that, even if you counted the angels, or numbered the Rulers, Thrones, and Authorities, even if you called to mind the Seraphim on high, you would surely agree (assuming that you were of sound mind) that they are greatly inferior to the very highest rank of glory. Such an honor is the highest available and must of necessity belong solely to the nature that rules the universe. So how could it be that someone who has been crucified could become the "Lord of Glory"? How could it be that he who is the "Father's reflection" and the "representation of his being," he who "bears all things

97. 1 Cor 2.6–8.
98. Heb 1.3–4.

by his powerful word" is said to have become greater than the angels? It is because, I would argue, when he became a man he accepted a status below theirs. For it is written, "We see Jesus, brought down a little lower than the angels, due to the suffering of death, crowned with glory and honor."[99] So are we to be made to strip the Word, who issues from God the Father, of the prominence that belongs to his being, and of his exact likeness to [the Father], just because he took a status that was lower than the glory of the angels on account of the condescension associated with God's plan of salvation? Not at all! I believe rather that we must neither completely disentangle the Word of God from the humanity after his convergence with the flesh, nor deprive the humanity of the glory that belongs properly to divinity, so long as we think and speak of this as being in Christ.

28. But I am sure there will be people who ask, "Who is Jesus Christ really? Is he a man born of a woman? Or is he God's Word?" It is a waste of effort even to bother repudiating such stuff and nonsense. I would say, though, that splitting man and Word into two separate parts is dangerous and will cause damage. It is excluded by soteriology, while the Holy Scriptures pronounce that Christ is one. I would myself assert that neither God's Word, while separate from the humanity, nor the temple born of a woman, when not united to the Word, can be called "Jesus Christ." For what we think of as Christ is God's Word after it has been ineffably brought together with the humanity in accordance with the saving union. He is above humanity since he is by nature God and Son, but at the same time the fact that he saw fit to bring himself down to the human level does him no dishonor. At one time he said, "Whoever has seen me has seen the Father; I and the Father are one,"[100] but then at another, that "the Father is greater than I."[101] It was for humanity's sake that he called himself inferior, even though he was not actually lesser than the Father since he is the same in terms of substance and in every way his equal.

---

99. Heb 2.9.   100. Jn 10.30.
101. Jn 14.28.

29. There are times when the Holy Scriptures speak of him as wholly a man while saying nothing about the divinity (because of the plan of salvation), and then there are also times when it speaks of him as God while saying nothing about the humanity. There is nothing misguided about this because the two have been conjoined into a unity. So then God's mouthpiece Paul, Hebrew of Hebrews, of the tribe of Benjamin,[102] called to be an apostle,[103] wrote as follows to those who had been justified through faith and had put to death the material aspects of life (I mean of course sexual immorality, passions, evil desires, and greed):[104] "For you have died, and your life is hidden with Christ in God."[105] Concerning his own disciples, Christ himself said, "Holy Father, keep them in your name which you gave me, so that they may be one as we are. While I was among them, I kept them in your name which you gave me, and I guarded them, and none have been lost, except the son of destruction— so that the Scripture might be fulfilled. But now, I am coming to you, and I say these things while I am in the world, so that they may have the joy which is mine made complete in them."[106] Do you understand that it is only the human aspects, those that we share, that are under consideration in these passages? But let us not think that he was somehow hidden or absent from the world, since he wisely says, "Truly I tell you that wherever two or three meet together in my name, there am I in the midst of them,"[107] and again, "Behold, I am with you all your days until the fulfillment of the age."[108] You see that even the most holy Paul frequently felt the need to avoid calling him a man; for example, he said, "Paul, apostle not from men or by men, but by Jesus Christ,"[109] and furthermore, "I am telling you that the gospel I preached is not a human thing, for I did not receive it from a man, nor was I taught it; rather, it came through a revelation from Jesus Christ."[110] And in another place he also says, "If we have known Christ according to the flesh, no lon-

102. Phil 3.5.
103. Rom 1.1.
104. Col 3.5.
105. Col 3.3.
106. Jn 17.11–13.
107. Mt 18.20.
108. Mt 28.20.
109. Gal 1.1.
110. Gal 1.11–12.

ger do we know him in that way."[111] Who, then, is this "Jesus
Christ," who struck Paul with such an ineffable and unerring
divine revelation of the mysteries about himself? Is he not the
Word made flesh, who for our sakes did not disdain being born
of a woman? Surely what I am saying is right! Do not forget what
blessed Gabriel said to the holy Virgin: "Do not be afraid, Mary;
behold, you shall conceive and bear a son, and you shall call
his name Jesus."[112] I would argue that this name that the Father
bestowed upon the Word via this message from the angel was a
new one, as that is just what the prophetic oracle had predicted:
"and they will call him by a new name, one which the Lord will
give."[113] So, when the Only-Begotten Son, co-eternal with the Father before all ages, became man in these later stages of world
history, was born of a woman,[114] was established as the Son, and
was even given the name of "firstborn" by becoming one among
many brothers,[115] at that time he who is by nature the Father
bestowed his name upon him on the basis, one might say, of a
father's rights.

30. So then, the same individual is at once both the Only-
Begotten and the firstborn. He is the former insofar as he is
God, and he is the firstborn insofar as he is one of us in the way
the saving union requires it, one among many brothers, a man.
The point of this was that we too, both in him and through him,
naturally and also by grace, might become God's children. We
become so naturally because we exist in him, and in him alone,
whereas we become so through him by the Spirit by participating
in his grace. Just as the condition of being the Only-Begotten,
which belongs especially to Christ, became a property of his humanity when the latter was united to the Word (a conjunction
that occurred in accordance with the plan of salvation), so also
in turn did the conditions of being "one among many brothers"
and of being the firstborn become properties of the Word after
being united to the flesh. Because his being God and his eternal
changelessness were firmly established, he remained just what

111. 2 Cor 5.16.   112. Lk 1.30.
113. Is 62.2.   114. Gal 4.4.
115. Rom 8.29.

he was even when he became a man who was crowned with the highest glory and transcendence. This is why the most sacred and blessed army of heavenly spirits has been commanded to worship him just as we do. You see, they would have had reason on their side if they had thought so little of the human condition as to shrink from affording him such honors when he became one of us for our sakes; they would have been scrupulously avoiding any guilt in considering him unworthy of such glory, even though he became like us for our sakes. You see, at that time they still could not understand the mystery about Christ until the Spirit revealed it to them rather than allowing these sacred beings to do anything impious. This is why Paul, who was God's mouthpiece, said, "When he brings the firstborn into the world he says, 'Let all the angels of God worship him.'"[116] So then, he whose natural property is to be quite other from the whole universe and who is external to it, came into it; as a man he became a part of it,[117] save only that he did not on this account abandon his divine glory. He is thus to be worshiped as the Only-Begotten, even as we call him the firstborn since that is a name admirably well-suited to human finiteness.

31. So are we worshiping Emmanuel as a man, then? Heaven forbid! That would be completely mad, deeply wrong. It would make us no different from those who worship created things instead of the Creator, "who exchanged the truth of God for a lie,"[118] as [Scripture] puts it. If we share in their way of thinking, then we will get back the exact same response they did: "Those claiming to be wise became fools and exchanged the glory of the incorruptible God for an image like corruptible man and like birds, animals, and reptiles."[119] If we were to offer our worship to Emmanuel as if he were just a regular person, someone exactly like us, would not we ourselves become just like these people, both in our actions and in our thoughts, by deceptively exchanging God's glory for an image of a corruptible man?

116. Heb 1.6.
117. "Part of the world": this seems to have been an anti-Apollinarian expression common to a number of Alexandrian authors.
118. Rom 1.25.
119. Rom 1.22–23.

Then what? Would not the very multitude of the angels above be implicated in this madness as well? Furthermore, I reckon this is the inescapable charge of perverseness that we can lay against the mass of the nations. The stigma of this age-old sin of theirs clings to them. You see, I would argue that they are just as much at fault as they ever were and they still have not recognized which is the right path. It seems superfluous that the blessed Paul addressed them thus: "but at that time, not knowing God, you were enslaved to those who by nature are not gods; but now that you know God, or rather are known by God, how can you turn again to the weak and poor elements, which you desire to be enslaved to all over again?"[120] After all, if the Christ that they have now believed in is not actually by nature God, then what sort of God had they come to know? If they have been worshiping a man, then they have fallen into the trap of the age-old sin. Is that not true? It must be. You see, then, Christ-loving Emperor, it is an assured result of incontrovertible logic, as well as being the wise thing to do, that we should worship the Word, who comes from God the Father, as being very God by nature, even though he looked just as we do, since the concurrence of the two into a unity is quite sufficient to dispel any suspicion that we may have been harboring about him being merely human. The Word's nature took the humanity to itself for sure, but he was not "merely" human. Instead, because his own glory overshadowed the element that he assumed, the Word permanently preserved his divine transcendence without confusing it with the humanity. This is what the disciples had realized when they worshiped him with the words, "Truly you are the Son of God,"[121] even though they could see him walking around in a human body; in reality, he was walking miraculously, as God.

32. An opponent of this doctrine might ask, "Who was it, then, that said to the Samaritan woman, 'You worship what you do not know, but we worship what we do know'?[122] and how can we categorize the worshiped together with the worshipers?" But

120. Gal 4.8–9.   121. Mt 14.33.
122. Jn 4.22.

this question of "who" is a very stupid and ignorant one, since it can only refer to the whole Christ. There is no division. He who conversed with the woman was the one and only Lord Jesus Christ, he who is composed from a humanity which enacts worship and a divinity which is worshiped. To put it another way, it is he who genuinely has both God's being and his name, and has a man's as well. Insofar as he is God, he himself is to be reckoned as the Lord of Glory; insofar as he is the one who became a man and who has been glorified by God through participation, he asks for this glory by saying, "Father, glorify your Son."[123] It is also written, however, that "there is one Lord, one faith, one baptism,"[124] and so just as there is a single faith, that is, in Christ, and also only really a single baptism, although we are baptized and believe in Father, Son, and Holy Spirit, so in the same way and for the same reason there is a single worship, namely, that of the Father, of the incarnate Son, and of the Holy Spirit. The Only-Begotten, even when he became flesh, dwelt among us, and was called the firstborn among many brothers, was never deprived of that worship that both we and the holy angels owe him. What further basis can there be for faith in him? Surely this is wholly justifiable. I do not believe that anyone in his right mind would suggest that we have stripped the flesh from the Word that comes from God the Father and then have worshiped the latter on its own.[125] Let us not miss the chance to say it yet again (since I have said it before), that our faith is not directed at one of our own, towards a man, but towards God, who really is by nature to be found "in Christ's person," a point with which the wise Paul was in total agreement when he wrote that "we do not preach ourselves, but Jesus Christ as Lord, and ourselves as your servants for Jesus Christ's sake. For God who said, Let light shine out of darkness, has shone into our hearts to make the knowledge of his glory in Christ's person visible."[126]

123. Jn 17.1.
124. Eph 4.5.
125. The image of the pre-incarnate Word as being like a soul that was "naked" before being "clothed" with the body goes back to Philo and depends upon a common philosophical conception.
126. 2 Cor 4.5–6. "Person" (*prosopon*): Paul really means "face" rather than

You can see just how clearly this light, which gives us our knowledge of God the Father, shines in Christ's person, and that is why he also could say, "Whoever has seen me has seen the Father; I and the Father are one."[127]

33. The divine representation, however, is not something material, but something that exists only within a peculiarly divine power and glory; in Christ, this is found in its purest form. He thought it appropriate, however, that he should be recognized not just by saying things like this, but he also wanted to exalt the minds of his listeners through the extraordinary nature of what he did, although his visible body made him out to be pathetic in the eyes of those who did not understand. "If I do not do my Father's works, then do not believe in me; but if I do, and you still do not believe, then believe in my works."[128] I think that Christ said this at the time because he knew that the saying would turn out to be rather appropriate. You see, there were some who thought that he who became a man for us was not actually God by nature, but that he was just a regular person like one of us, and so they made out that it was unacceptable to put one's faith in him. All their uncertainty and hesitation needed to be cut away and their faith directed towards his divine nature, as if it were the very person of the Father, rather than attributing it to human baseness; hence he said that "the one who believes in me believes not in me but in the one who sent me, and the one who sees me sees the one who sent me."[129] It was as if he had said, "You who are listening to what I am saying, do not have a low opinion of me, like something you have picked off the ground; you should know rather that by placing your faith in me when you see me physically, you are not just placing your faith in a human being, but, through me, you are placing it in the very Father himself; as his Son, I am his equal in every way, even though I have been made flesh for your sake and have taken the base cloak of humanity as my dwelling-place, while

"person," but by Cyril's day the term was a technical one for the person of Christ, and that is how he takes it here in the Pauline citation.

127. Jn 14.9; 10.30.   128. Jn 10.37–38.
129. Jn 12.44.

still retaining undiminished the equality of nature and action that we share, and remaining in exactly the same state of glory."

34. To look at it from another direction, you may be assured that Christ does not reject faith, but rather that he accepts faith in his own person, just so long as it involves no division or distinction, even after the Incarnation. To see what I mean, think of the healing of the man born blind. Christ infused into him a light that was both sweet and unwonted, and quite understandably everyone was truly shocked. After he had been set free from his condition, the Jews interrogated him as to who the healer was, and when Christ later came across him he asked, "Do you believe in the Son of God?"[130] The other cried out, "Who is he, Lord, that I may believe in him?" Christ replied, "You have seen him, and it is he who is speaking with you," and the man then said, "'I believe, Lord,' and worshiped him."[131] Yet is it not a fact universally acknowledged that the divine and transcendent nature is wholly invisible, since the Scripture says, "Nobody has ever seen God"?[132] But had he meant to separate off his humanity and elicit faith in the Word of God the Father, stripped naked, so to speak, and on its own, then why did he not command the healed man to consider that it was the divine nature? Instead of this he focused on his materiality, on what was visible to the eyes, by saying, "You have seen him, and it is he who is speaking with you." Surely we should admit that he is referring here to his body? Otherwise, in what sense could one think of him as being his flesh unless one thinks of him as being identical with what he made his own by entering into a union with it? It is just the same, of course, when we consider ourselves. Even if someone referred just to the flesh, one would not thereby be intending to give an incomplete or merely partial description of our humanity, that is, our soul and body together.

35. On one occasion the wise John wrote for us that "Jesus also did many other signs in front of his disciples, which are not written in this book; these ones are written so that you may believe that Jesus is the Christ, the Son of God, and that, by be-

---

130. Jn 9.35.   131. Jn 9.35–38.
132. Jn 1.18.

lieving, you may have eternal life in his name."[133] What God's mouthpiece Peter publicly declared to the Jews is just as incredible: "Leaders and elders of the people, if we are being examined today because of a good deed for a sick man, as to how he was healed, know this, all of you and all the people of Israel, that it was in the name of Jesus Christ of Nazareth, whom you crucified, but whom God raised from the dead—in that [name] does this man stand before you healed."[134] And then after that, "Salvation is in no one else, for there is no other name given under heaven for men by which we must be saved."[135] Who is this one who suffered death, who was raised up in glory, and who came from Nazareth, if he be not Jesus Christ, that is, he who was ineffably begotten from the Father before the ages, but more recently, in the last age, when the end of the world is on its way, has also been physically born from a woman? And so anyone who places his faith in him will receive in return a great privilege, for he will be called God's child. "However many as received him, to those who would believe in his name, he gave them the power to become God's children, those born not of blood, nor of physical desire, nor human desire, but of God."[136]

36. "So that he might be first in all things," "he was born of a woman,"[137] but since, through his sacred status, he is the firstfruits of the divinely transformed creation, he was also proved to have been born of the Spirit before all other things. He never had anything to do with the sexual union of man and woman, though he did not condemn that natural act as being dishonorable (after all, "marriage is honorable," and "the Creator at the beginning made them as male and female").[138] Instead, he brought what was human together with something incomparably superior. He wanted us no longer to be reckoned as the children of men, but of the Spirit. After all, he said, "Call none on earth your father; for you have one Father in heaven, and you are all brothers."[139] So how could believing in this individual be in any way open to criticism? On the contrary, such faith

---

133. Jn 20.30.
135. Acts 4.12.
137. Gal 4.4; Col 1.18.
139. Mt 23.9, 8.

134. Acts 4.8–10.
136. Jn 1.12–13.
138. Heb 13.4; Mt 19.4.

receives the reward of sins forgiven. The discerning Paul makes the same point: "Knowing that no man is justified by the works of the Law, but only by faith in Jesus Christ, we have believed in Christ Jesus, so that we may be justified" in him.[140] I do not at all shrink from saying all over again what I said previously, that Christ Jesus is not to be thought of as God's Word, stripped naked and on his own. On the contrary, once he had taken up the humanity, and once he had woven the flesh to himself without confusing the two, it was then, precisely when he existed in a visible state and with a human form, that the Father revealed him to the holy apostles by issuing a heavenly proclamation that said, "This is my beloved Son, in whom I am pleased; listen to him."[141] You must appreciate that he did not say, "My son is within this individual," precisely so that we would think of him as being one and the same individual, in the context of a union that brings salvation, and not in terms of parts or as if there were one thing within another. John convinces us that it is sinful, indeed extremely dangerous, to believe otherwise; he wrote, "because this is the testimony of God, which he has testified concerning his Son. The one who believes in God's Son has God's testimony within him; the one who does not believe in the Son makes him out to be a liar, because he has not believed in the testimony, which God has testified to concerning his Son."[142] In fact, what he testified was that this individual, who exists together with his flesh and in a servant's form, is indeed his very own unique and special Son. We shall surely concede that the wonderful grace that comes through holy baptism, the fact of becoming alive in him, and the possibility of participating in God through the Spirit's sanctification, are all brought about by Jesus Christ. Remember what John said: "He who comes after me is greater than I, who am not sufficient to carry his sandals; he will baptize you in the Holy Spirit and fire."[143] Can we really say that to be baptized in the Holy Spirit and in fire could be the work of humanity? How could it ever be so? John spoke of a man who was not as yet present or visible but who would come and baptize in fire and in the Holy Spirit, not by infusing into

140. Gal 2.16.   141. Mt 17.5.
142. 1 Jn 5.9–10.   143. Mt 3.11.

the baptized some spirit that did not belong to him, as if he were just rendering a service, but a Spirit that comes from him and that belongs to him by divine authority, seeing as he is God by nature, a Spirit by which the divine image might also be imprinted upon us. For we are being transformed, as it were, into the divine image, into Christ Jesus, not by being re-configured into a body again (that would be a simplistic way of looking at it), but by being given a share in the Holy Spirit we come to possess Christ himself within ourselves. That is why we show our joy by crying out, "My soul rejoices in the Lord, for he clothed me with a cloak of salvation and a tunic of gladness."[144] He says, "Whichever of you has been baptized into Christ have clothed yourselves with Christ."[145]

37. At this point, someone might interrupt us to ask, "Is it the case, then, that we have been baptized into a man? Is that not really how it is?" Well, he will feel our riposte: "Silence, man, what do you think you are doing? Smashing our hopes to the ground?" You see, we have not simply been baptized into some man, but into the God-made-man, into him who frees from their punishment and from their former sins any who have accepted faith in him. This is why Peter, God's mouthpiece, urged the Jews to "repent and be baptized, each one of you, in the name of Jesus Christ for the forgiveness of your sins, and you will receive the gift of the Holy Spirit."[146] For in cleansing of their sin all who entreat him, he anoints them with his very own Spirit. In his role as God the Father's Word, he infuses this Spirit and causes it to well up within us from his very own nature, whereas in his role as a man he physically breathed it out in a perfectly ordinary way, doing so for the sake of the salvific purpose of the Incarnation and on account of the union, for he breathed onto the holy apostles and said, "Receive the Holy Spirit."[147] John says that "he gives the Spirit without measure,"[148] but it is from his very self that he imparts it, in just the same way that the Father does. That is why Paul, God's mouthpiece, avoids making any real distinc-

144. Is 61.10.
145. Gal 3.27.
146. Acts 2.38.
147. Jn 20.22.
148. Jn 3.34.

tion here and sometimes seems to attribute the Spirit to God the Father, and at other times to the Son. For example, he writes, "You are not in the flesh but in the Spirit, if the Spirit of God lives in you. If anyone does not have the Spirit of Christ, such a person does not belong to him; whereas if Christ is in you, even though the body is dead because of sin, the spirit lives because of righteousness."[149] It was appropriate, then, to say that the Spirit belongs especially to the Son, not just insofar as he is the Father's Word, but just as much when one considers him as being made a man as we are, leaving to one side the divine characteristics that belong to his own nature. This is also the reason why we can say that he has been made alive just as we have, even though he is himself the source of life for everything because of his being ineffably born from the living Father. One can nevertheless see that he has graced his own flesh with the glory that belongs to divine activity, but that at the same time he has also made material things his own, as if he had wrapped them around his very own nature, in accordance with the salvation-bringing union.

38. Someone's now going to ask, "Is it really right that he is actually by nature God the Father's Word to descend from heaven and to have the power to grant life to whatever things he wants to receive it?" Well, would anyone seriously try to suggest that the divine ability to create is a human faculty? Of course not! How can it be that, as God, he grants us life, and this not merely by making us partakers of the Holy Spirit, but by actually offering us the flesh that he assumed as something to eat? For he said, "Truly, truly I say to you, if you do not eat the flesh of the Son of Man, and drink his blood, then you have no life in yourselves."[150] There was one occasion when the Jews were railing against him and debating as to who was the greatest. They somehow suggested that it was the blessed Moses and publicly said, "Our fathers ate manna in the desert, as it is written: 'He gave them bread from heaven to eat.' What sign will you give that we should believe in you?"[151] If, as you claim, you have brought your body down from above, out of heaven, then what

149. Rom 8.9–10. 150. Jn 6.53.
151. Jn 6.31, 30.

will you do to prove it? He replied, "Truly, truly, I say to you that Moses did not give you the true bread that comes from heaven; for the bread of God is the one that comes down from heaven and gives life to the world."[152] Furthermore, he even pointed directly at himself and showed that he was embodied by saying, "I am the living bread who comes down from heaven; anyone who eats of this bread will live forever, and the bread which I give is my flesh, for the life of the world. The one who eats my flesh and drinks my blood remains in me, and I in him. Just as the Father who sent me lives, so I also live because of the Father, and the one who eats me will live because of me."[153] And yet, surely his flesh did not actually come down from heaven as such, but came from the Virgin just as the Scriptures say it did? There are all sorts of ways of proving conclusively that it is not the Word as such that is eaten, but rather it is insofar as he has brought the properties of the two natures together into a single individual, a conjunction that was designed to bring salvation. Now Nicodemus did not understand this mystery, and so in his confusion he cried out, "How can this be?" He replied, "If I speak to you of earthly things and you do not believe, how then will you believe if I speak to you of heavenly things? Nobody has gone up into heaven, except the one who came down from heaven, the Son of Man."[154] But then there were Jews who suffered from the same lack of sense as Nicodemus and who decided to mock him (how could they!) for claiming that his own body was life-giving and came from heaven. To these he asked, "Does this offend you? What if you were to see the Son of Man going up to where he was before?"[155] Surely we agree that the Emmanuel was born of a woman? In which case, given that the body that was united to him had indeed been born of the holy Virgin, where can he have been beforehand, or how could he possibly say that he would return there? For sure, we must concede that it is impossible for an earthly body to have the power to give life, at least insofar as it exists in its own nature? Tell me, then, how could it be that flesh can give life? How can what is of earthly origin also

152. Jn 6.32–33.   153. Jn 6.51, 56–57.
154. Jn 3.9, 12–13.   155. Jn 6.61–62.

be reckoned as being from heaven? Surely the answer is that [these things can be true] because of the union that pertains to the living, heavenly Word. This, I would argue, is the doctrine that is most orthodox and which best accords with the Scriptures. Even when he is being considered in his incarnate state, he is still not other than the divine Creator.

39. I shall again make Paul, who is God's mouthpiece, an accomplice to my argument. He wrote as follows: "giving thanks to the Father, who has qualified us to share in the inheritance of the saints in light, who has rescued us from the dominion of darkness and brought us into the kingdom of his beloved Son, in whom we have redemption, the forgiveness of sins. This Son is the image of the invisible God, the firstborn of all creation, because in him all things were created, things in heaven and on earth, visible and invisible, whether thrones or powers or rulers or authorities; all things have been created through him and for him; and he is before all things, and in him all things hold together. He is the head of the body, the church; he is the beginning and the firstborn from among the dead, so that in everything he might have the supremacy, since God was pleased to have all his fullness dwell in him, and through him to reconcile to himself all things, by making peace through the blood of his cross, whether things on earth or things in heaven."[156] See how clearly [Paul] says that all things were created through him and for him, and also that he is before all things and that all things hold together in him. It also says that he is the firstborn from among the dead, and that he brought peace to things in heaven and on earth through his blood. Who is this "firstborn from among the dead" but Christ Jesus, that is, the Word both in the flesh, together with his flesh? For insofar as his own nature is concerned, as God the Word he could never die, while as a common human being he could hardly be reckoned as the Creator of everything, unless of course it was as God that he enacted creation (so long as one does not think of him without his flesh at any time subsequent to the union), while it was insofar as he appeared as a human being that he was the firstborn

156. Col 1.12–20.

from among the dead (albeit not laying aside his being God on account of the Incarnation).

40. You can see in other passages how the inspired authors confirm these exact points. For example, John says, "In the beginning was the Word, and the Word was with God, and the Word was God. He was with God in the beginning. Through him all things were made; without him nothing was made that has been made,"[157] while Paul says that "there is one God the Father, from whom are all things, and one Lord Jesus Christ through whom are all things."[158] But if there had been some gulf between the Word and the flesh after their being united to each other, or were there any sort of division into separate items, such as into two sons as some people reckon, then how could all things have been created through Jesus Christ? Yet all things were created through him. It is evident, then, that he retained what properly and by nature belongs to God's Word even after he became a man. Even to think about making a division is to stand on a precipice, for the Lord Jesus Christ is one, and through him the Father created all things. As God, therefore, he is Creator and as Life he is Life-Giver, composed out of both human and supra-human properties into one in-between sort of thing.[159] After all, the Scriptures say that there is a "mediator between God and men,"[160] who is by nature God, albeit not apart from his flesh, and who is also genuinely a man, but not a "mere" man like one of us, since he remained just what he was as well as becoming flesh. After all, it is written that "Jesus Christ is the same yesterday and today and forever."[161]

41. Do we not, after all, believe that in these last stages of history Emmanuel was born through the holy and god-bearing Virgin? Surely this is just what we believe. Now this "yesterday and

157. Jn 1.1–3.

158. 1 Cor 8.6.

159. This intriguing expression became the subject of intense debate about Miaphysite circles in the sixth century; see Iain R. Torrance, *Christology after Chalcedon: Severus of Antioch and Sergius the Monophysite* (Norwich: Canterbury Press, 1988), 159.

160. 1 Tm 2.5.

161. Heb 13.8.

today," O Christ-loving Emperor, seems to me to refer to the present and the past. If that is the case, then how can he have been "the same" individual in the past before he had come into his fleshly existence? Well, the Word existed in the beginning and was himself eternal and unchanging in his own nature precisely because he was fathered by an eternal and unchanging God. Yet has not this name, Jesus Christ, been used to denote the Word only in more recent times, in fact since the time of the Incarnation? Yes, that is indeed so, as we have already demonstrated in all sorts of ways.[162] Now, take into consideration that he is saying that this individual who is the same yesterday and today and forever is Christ Jesus, and not just the Word on his own. So how is it, then, that a human nature may remain unchanged and possess continuity of identity even while experiencing change, specifically change from non-being to being and life? Have the Holy Scriptures in fact lied to us by telling us that something pre-existed which did not even exist yesterday? I, for one, would certainly not say that, not at all! Jesus Christ is the same yesterday, today, and forever. I will never deny the Word's antiquity and permanence, despite his becoming flesh; instead I would suggest that it is because of the union with his own flesh that he can be referred to as having existed yesterday, that is, to have pre-existence. It is true that the deranged Jew loathed him and tried to stone him because he would not believe it. That witless Jew who tore him to pieces because he refused to believe him and prepared to stone him, was shocked precisely because, although he looked like a regular man like any other, he claimed that he was older than any man; they had said to him, "You are not yet fifty years old, and you have seen Abraham?" and so, as God, he replied, "Truly, truly, I say to you that before Abraham was, I am."[163] John also says, "This is the one about whom I said, 'After me comes a man who is in front of me because he existed before me.'"[164] If John knew that Christ was a man (hence calling him Emmanuel), how could he then say that someone who was younger than he and hence "after him" was actually "in front of him" and "existed before

162. See §36.   163. Jn 8.58.
164. Jn 1.30.

him"? You might answer, "As I understand it, when he says that 'he is in front of me and existed before me,' he is thinking in terms of degrees of honor." All right then, but a very brief point will allow me to show that suggestion to be wholly false. If we allow that the words "in front of" refer to having a greater degree of honor, then by the same argument we would have to say that the term "after" surely denotes what comes second in importance. It then follows of necessity that we should, quite foolishly, suppose Christ to be less glorious than John and to have come after him, since he said that "a man is coming after me." What an absurd thing to suggest! This is certainly not our opinion, especially considering what the Psalms say: "Who among the clouds shall be equal to the Lord? Who among God's children shall be likened to the Lord?"[165] It follows that we must attribute to Christ the greater age, even after his Incarnation, since he is by nature God, united to flesh, and because he ordinarily causes the virtues of his own nature to be held in common with those which pertain to his own body.

42. This being the case, then, and being accurately expressed, you could very easily go on and discover the same thing from other sources. There is a place where God spoke through one of his holy prophets concerning the Christ who comes from the seed of David according to the flesh: "And you, Bethlehem, house of Ephratha, you are few in number among the thousands of Judah; for from you will come forth to me one who is to be a ruler over Israel; his coming was from the very beginning, from the days of eternity."[166] The holy Paul said about those Israelites that "they were all baptized into Moses in the cloud and in the sea. They all ate the same spiritual food and drank the same spiritual drink; for they drank from the spiritual rock that accompanied them, and that rock was Christ."[167] Surely he is here adjudging that the great antiquity that belongs properly to the Word is to be found in Christ Jesus, in the context of the salvific union. That is clear enough, is it not? He says most specifically that he who came from Bethlehem, insofar as he is a man born

165. Ps 89.6 (88.7 LXX).   166. Mi 5.2.
167. 1 Cor 10.2–4.

of a woman, came forth from the very beginning. For the Word-made-man existed in the very beginning, before time, and he was himself the rock that quenched Israel's thirst with streams of water that they had not at all been expecting, and this even though in the later stages of history he was born, became a human being, and was anointed by God the Father to send his message out into the world. It is only for the latter reason that he is called Christ, and yet, as Paul says, Christ was also the rock.[168] The wise John reinforces this point as well, and strengthens it by not merely allowing the natures to sit alongside one another, but by binding together the functions of the properties that pertain to each. Look at how he puts it: "That which was from the beginning, which we have heard, which we have seen with our eyes, which we have looked at and our hands have touched—this we proclaim concerning the Word of life. The life appeared; we have seen it and testify to it, and we proclaim to you the eternal life, which was with the Father and has appeared to us."[169] See how he states quite definitely that he who is from the beginning is both visible and tangible. After he had traced out with his finger the side of Christ's body and the lacerations from the nails, Thomas cried out, "My Lord and my God."[170] Saint Luke could also say that the holy apostles had become eyewitnesses and servants of the Word because the incorporeal had become visible and the intangible tangible, not in the sense that his flesh was like some foreign earthly garment, but because he had made it into his very own temple and because he was being revealed as both God and Lord in and with that flesh. You know, do you not, that the holy Paul wrote somewhere that "none of us lives to himself alone, and none of us dies to himself alone. If we live, we live to the Lord; and if we die, we die to the Lord. So, whether we live or die, we belong to the Lord. For this very reason, Christ died and returned to life so that he might be the Lord of both the dead and the living."[171]

168. This sentence is absent from the ancient Syriac translation and may be a scribal gloss.

169. 1 Jn 1.1–2. 170. Jn 20.28.

171. Rom 14.7–9.

43. We have established, then, that he was made "Lord of both the dead and the living," simply and only because he himself died and was raised to life, and whom else but the Son would we ever describe as undergoing death and then coming back to life? I am sure everyone would agree that nobody else could be so described. What follows from this? Should we conclude that the Word of God the Father is mortal, subject to corruption, or that as Life he is beyond death, superior to corruption? Yet it is abundantly clear to everyone that, as Life, he is superior to death. If that is so, then how can he be both "among the dead" and "free," as the Scriptures have it?[172] For there is no way that the Word could, on his own account, die. Hence we formulate it this way: that his flesh actually died while he himself suffered.[173] After all, he is not separate from his flesh; he who, in terms of the law of matter and nature, died and was then raised, actually exists within his flesh and has bound to it the glory of his lordship. He thereby proved that death was a peculiarly human experience while resurrection was a work of God. The result of these two aspects is that we know him to be one of us and also, as God, above us; we envision him as the Lord of the universe, a position he held together with his own Father even before the Incarnation. Hence when Nathaniel recognized him, he said, "Rabbi, you are the Son of God; you are the King of Israel."[174] To his disciples he himself said, "You call me lord and teacher, and you are right, for that is what I am."[175] He backed this up by what he did, by forgiving sins and "granting power over unclean spirits, to drive them out, and to heal every sickness and every disease among the people."[176] For it was in the name of Jesus Christ of Nazareth that the man with the crippled foot, who sat at the Beautiful Gate, was healed. And Aeneas was able to shake off his chronic condition and escape a totally incurable illness because Peter, God's mouthpiece, said, "Aeneas, Jesus Christ heals you."

172. Ps 88.5 (87.5 LXX).
173. I.e., the flesh really died, while the Word felt the pain of death without actually dying.
174. Jn 1.50.   175. Jn 13.13.
176. Acts 3.6, 2.

44. So then, because we are driving towards the truth in every direction, because we are absolutely passionate about following the path mapped out by the Holy Scriptures, and because we are in line with the opinions of the Fathers, we may conclude that the individual who came from Jesse's root and from David's seed, the individual who came from a woman according to the flesh, and who, as a man, is as subject to the law as we are (while as God he is above both us and the law), who was "among the dead" like us and for us, who is himself able to bestow heavenly life upon us and who actually is Life, it is this individual who is really, genuinely the Son of God. We do not strip his humanity of its divinity nor divest the Word of his humanity after the ineffable and inconceivable union. Instead, we confess the one individual Son, who ineffably manifested himself as a single individual composed out of both these elements; and to be sure, this happened by a union made in heaven, not by some transformation in his nature.

45. Christ's disciple makes clear just how great a profit accrues to those who hold this position when he says that "whoever confesses that Jesus is the Son of God, God remains in him and he in God."[177] The statement that "the Word became flesh and made his dwelling among us"[178] proves that Jesus Christ, he who is from David's seed according to the flesh, is also really by nature the Son of God, and the wise John further confirms this by saying that "we know also that the Son of God has come and has given us understanding, so that we may know the true God. And we are in him who is true, in his Son Jesus Christ. He is the one that is the true God and is eternal life,"[179] by whom and with whom be glory to God the Father, with the Holy Spirit, forever and ever. Amen.

177. 1 Jn 4.15.   178. Jn 1.14.
179. 1 Jn 5.20.

A DEFENSE OF THE TWELVE
ANATHEMAS AGAINST THEODORET

Theodoret's Letter to John of Antioch[1]

HEN I LOOKED at those anathemas that you sent me and asked me to refute in writing so as to make clear for everyone in what sense they were heretical, I was rather shocked. I was shocked that a man who was appointed as shepherd, who was entrusted with an enormous flock, and who was ordained to heal the sick sheep among them, is mentally unhinged, seriously so, and is also trying to infect his lambs with his disease and treats his sheep more harshly even than wild beasts do. Wild beasts scatter the flock and then pick off the ones that have become separated, but this man is right in their midst and is reckoned to be a savior and protector, all the while furtively leading astray those who have trusted him. One can defend against an open attack, but against a treacherous attack made under the guise of friendship one is defenseless and will doubtless receive injury. Hence traitors within are more dangerous than foes without.

I am even more annoyed that he is making all these heretical

1. *Letter* 150. The sequence of items in the *Against Theodoret* appears confusing at first glance but reflects how the conversation was transmitted in the official reports of the council. The dossier opens with Theodoret's *Letter* 150 (probably to be dated to February 431), written after he has received from his metropolitan, John of Antioch, a copy of Cyril's anathemas together with a request to pen a response. This is followed in the dossier by Theodoret's discussion of the first anathema, and only after this do we get the opening remarks of Cyril's riposte, addressed in the form of a letter to Euoptius, outlining what he plans to do after reading Theodoret's comments. His response to Theodoret on the subject of the first anathema then follows. The rest of the text follows the regular pattern of quoting the anathema itself, then "the heretic's refutation," followed by Cyril's defense.

and blasphemous statements in the name of true religion and under the shepherd's dignity. He is simply repeating again the meaningless, and also profane, doctrines of Apollinarius, which were stamped out long ago. To cap it off he is not merely supporting these doctrines, but also daring to pronounce anathemas against anyone who is not prepared to share his blasphemy. This is all, of course, supposing that these productions are genuine rather than being written in his name by some enemy of the truth who has thrown an apple into our midst, as the old story has it, so as to fan the flame of discord as high as possible.[2]

In any case, whether it was he himself or someone else who wrote all this, I have myself composed a refutation as well as I could, given God's help in furnishing me with the Holy Spirit's aid so as to investigate this hare-brained heresy. I have set against it the teachings of the evangelists and apostles. I have shown how his dogma is totally unnatural and miles away from God's teaching, and by comparing it with what the Holy Spirit says I have shown just how little his ideas have in common with God's.

Against these reckless anathemas, I will retort that Paul was yelling the truth like a herald when he pronounced an anathema against those who had corrupted the teachings of evangelists and apostles.[3] He even dared pronounce it against the angels, but not against those who kept within the bounds laid down by the theologians, whom he instead fortified with blessings: "May peace and mercy be upon all those who walk according to this rule, especially on the Israel of God."[4] May, then, the author of these writings enjoy the fruits of his own work and the harvest of his heretical seeds and feel the force of the Apostle's curse, while we stay within the teachings of the holy Fathers.

I have appended to this letter my counter-arguments. You may read them and so decide whether I have effectively deconstructed his heretical formulae. I have written down each anath-

---

2. A reference to the Greek myth of the wedding of Peleus and Thetis, at which the uninvited goddess Discord (Eris) throws a golden apple in among the guests, declaring that the apple belongs to whoever is the fairest. The strife and discord she was able to arouse among the other goddesses present led to the Trojan War.

3. Gal 1.8.

4. Gal 6.16.

ema and then added the counter-argument, so that my readers might the more easily understand and so that the refutation of these dogmas might be clear.

Theodoret's Critique of the First Anathema

"If any do not confess Emmanuel to be truly God and, on this basis, the holy Virgin to be the Mother-of-God (since she bore in the flesh the Word of God made flesh), let them be anathema."[5]

We, however, who adhere to the evangelists' teaching would deny both that God the Word naturally became flesh and that he was transformed into flesh, since the divine is totally without change. This is why the prophet David says, "You are the same, and your years will not end."[6] That great herald of the truth Paul taught in Hebrews that this prophecy was made in reference to the Son.[7] Elsewhere God says through the prophet, "I am the Lord, and I do not change."[8] So if what is divine is wholly without change, it can never have experienced any change or alteration, and if what is without change cannot be changed, then God the Word did not become flesh by changing into it. Instead he took flesh and dwelt among us, as the evangelist says. Godly Paul makes this quite clear in Philippians: "May you have the same attitude as did Christ Jesus, who, although he was in God's form, did not intend to grasp at equality with God; instead he made himself nothing by taking a servant's form."[9]

Now, these verses make it clear that God's form remained what it was and took a servant's form rather than being actually changed into one. So if God the Word took upon himself living and rational flesh rather than actually becoming flesh, then he was not, in his nature, born of the Virgin, neither was he so conceived, molded, or formed, nor did he who existed as God before the ages, who is with God, and is known and worshiped together with the Father, derive from her the beginning of his existence; rather, he molded a temple for himself in the Virgin's womb, and existed together with what was molded, conceived,

---

5. This is Cyril's first anathema.   6. Ps 102.27 (101.28 LXX).
7. Heb 1.12.   8. Mal 3.6.
9. Phil 2.5–7.

formed, and born. It is for this reason that we too call the holy Virgin "Mother-of-God," not because she gave birth to him who is God by nature, but because she gave birth to a man who was united to the God that had created him. Further, if what was molded in the Virgin's womb was not man but God the Word, who existed before the ages, then God the Word would be the Holy Spirit's creation, since Gabriel says that "what is begotten within you is of the Holy Spirit."[10]

Yet, if the Only-Begotten Word of God was not created and is consubstantial and co-eternal with the Father, then he cannot be the Spirit's creation, and if it was not God the Word that was molded in the Virgin's womb by the Holy Spirit, then it follows that we should understand that what was molded, conceived, formed, and born was the servant's form. Now since this latter was not stripped of God's form, but was a temple which had God the Word living within it, just as Paul says ("for it pleased him that his whole fullness should dwell corporeally within him"),[11] so we too can address the Virgin as "Mother-of-God," not just as "mother of man." The latter title refers to what was molded, formed, and conceived, whereas the former refers to the union.

This is also why we name the child who was born Emmanuel, who is neither God separated from human nature, nor a man stripped of divinity. As the Gospels say, Emmanuel means "God with us," and this expression indicates that he is one of us who, for our sakes, was "taken," and it also speaks of God the Word who did the "taking." So then, it is because of God, who took [the man] upon himself, that the child is called Emmanuel, and it is because God's form united with the conceived form of a servant that the Virgin is called "Mother-of-God." For God the Word was not changed into flesh. God's form took upon himself a servant's form.

Cyril's Letter to Euoptius

Cyril, to the most godly brother and fellow-servant Euopti-us, whom I long to see, greetings in the Lord. When I came

10. Mt 1.23.
11. Col 1.19; 2.9.

across what your reverence recently sent to me, I was gratified by how well-disposed you were towards me and how genuine must be your love in Christ.[12] I suppose it would be appropriate now to mention that what it says in Proverbs is true, that "a brother helped by a brother is like a strong city."[13] And it seems to me that this sort of expression of love is highly valued by the Holy Scriptures, and rightly so, since it is the fulfillment of the law,[14] is greatly superior to the other virtues, and is held in high esteem in the souls of the saints. Indeed, I would add that this love is not brought to fruition by mere spoken words, but by the testimony of real actions. When people see precious stones, the so-called "Indian gems," they wonder at them not on the basis of what has been written about them, but because of what they actually look like; and in just the same way, I think, does the radiant beauty of love shine out when it testifies to all the best people through good deeds themselves. Your reverence is showing that same love to me, treading in the footprints of the saints, and making their upright way of life redound to your own glory.

I have taken delivery of the volume you sent me (the one supposedly written against the anathemas by Theodoret, who comes from Cyrus—at least I think that is what they call that little rural outpost), and I intend to carry out what is now required of me. When I found out what it contained, I offered up songs of thanksgiving to God, though I also immediately exclaimed, "Lord, save my soul from wicked lips and from a treacherous tongue."[15] For I find myself denounced from every angle and receiving criticism on each and every one of those headings. I realize, as some well-known people have pointed out, that this opponent of mine is very ready with his words and that, even though he has garnered a great deal of information from the Holy Scriptures, he has totally misunderstood the meaning of the anathemas. So great is this misunderstanding that I can only assume that he is acting the ignoramus to please certain individuals so that he might seem to be criticizing me pointedly rather than [to appear] just like some trivial rustic. (Having said that, I

---

12. Cf. 2 Cor 8.8.   13. Prv 18.19.
14. Rom 13.10.   15. Ps 120.2 (119.2 LXX).

do not think there is anything in there that is going to be hard to deal with or any attack that cannot be met.)

But since it has become necessary for me to compose something short in response to him, lest anyone think that the accused has chosen to remain silent, I shall construct as short an *apologia* as may be. If his entire aim is to argue with us about divine mysteries, then he ought, well-trained as he is in the divinely inspired Scriptures, to be making use of them alone and to be constructing his discourse in a way that is appropriate to its sacred subject and not casting antiquated and foul myths into our midst. You see, he has thought to compare my own words to the mythical apple of discord[16]—perhaps as a way of promoting his own great wisdom, at which we too are quite bowled over, for it appears that he knows all about this apple of discord and about Paris son of Priam on account of his logical acuity and enormous learning. Let us leave aside such matters for now and get on with the task at hand.

❧ *First Anathema*

If any do not confess Emmanuel to be truly God and, on this basis, the holy Virgin to be the Mother-of-God (since she bore in the flesh the Word of God made flesh), let them be anathema.

Cyril's Defense

I have loudly shouted down any who would shy away from confessing Emmanuel to be truly God and the holy Virgin to be the Mother-of-God, seeing as, when the Word of God became flesh, that is, a man, she gave birth to him according to flesh. If the one who is making accusations against this orthodox statement really thinks that Emmanuel is not truly God, or if he really thinks that it was not according to flesh that the holy Virgin gave birth to the Word of God when he became flesh, as the Scriptures have it, then why does he not clearly say so? What are you up to, my friend? You are spewing out some horrible

16. See n. 2 on p. 84 above in this chapter.

blasphemies and wantonly opposing orthodox dogma by suggesting that Emmanuel is not truly God nor is the holy Virgin the Mother-of-God.[17]

By comparing carefully what the divinely inspired Scriptures say as against the arguments this fellow is ranting about, and by setting against him both the tradition of apostolic and evangelical faith and the confession of the Fathers who once gathered at Nicaea, we have become convinced, not so much that he is dishonestly attacking my own words, but that in so doing he is really launching a shameless attack upon the whole of divine Scripture. But this wise and shrewd interpreter simply passed over what he really ought to have been discussing, thought nothing at all of dealing with these issues first, and instead set out on a quite different path. He turned straightaway to the crucial point, namely, that the Word of God is superior to change and did not alter into the nature of flesh, a point upon which the present anathema is quite firm and the truth of which it is trying to demonstrate.

Well then, let him hear this, since he is totally clueless when he reads these expressions that he opposes: you are totally off the point, my friend, and you are battling against an idea that we, too, find despicable. We know perfectly well that the divine, transcendent nature cannot experience any "shadow of turning,"[18] nor did the Word of God give up being what he is to be transformed into a fleshly nature. Since he points out that God's form took upon himself the form of a servant, let him go on and explain whether it was just these "forms" that came together by themselves, quite apart from their concrete existences. Well, I reckon that even he would shrink from saying that, for it was not mere resemblances and forms, things with no concrete existence, that conjoined together to bring about the saving union;

17. This is clearly meant to be a "quotation" from Theodoret. The latter did not use these words, but in the final paragraph of his critique he acknowledged the use of the terms "Emmanuel" and "Mother-of-God" only in a qualified sense; the implication is that Theodoret would not allow for the plain statements, "Emmanuel is God" and "the Virgin is the Mother-of-God." Hence Cyril is trying to elicit the real essence of Theodoret's position, which he saw as tantamount to Nestorius's explicit rejection of the title "Mother-of-God."

18. Jas 1.17.

rather, it was a convergence of the very things themselves, of two concrete existences. Then we can really have faith that a genuine incarnation took place.

So, if we do say, "The Word became flesh," then we do not mean by this a confusion or a mixing, nor a change or alteration, but rather that, in a way that cannot be fully described, he was united with a holy body that possessed a rational soul. The parts that were united cannot be said to be confused, but rather the one took the other into itself. What we affirm, then, is that the Word of God the Father took upon himself the holy and animate flesh and was truly united to it without confusion, and that he then came forth from the womb as a man, while also remaining truly God. It is on this basis that we call the holy Virgin "Mother-of-God."

Yet I think it is quite excessive to suggest that we should also call her "Mother-of-the-man."[19] Had there been some people foolishly suggesting that the Word's nature was like a source and that he only began to exist as such when he took the flesh, then there might have been some sort of argument that was not especially objectionable in favor of those willing to call her also the "Mother-of-the-man." But since such a premise is wholly detestable to all concerned and nobody would disagree that the holy Virgin should be reckoned as Mother-of-God—so long as one accepts the belief that the Word of God the Father became flesh, that is, a man (after all, as I have said, the Virgin certainly did not bring forth divinity on its own)—then what point is there in insisting that she be called "Mother-of-the-man"? It appears, however, that they actually used this device against Christ, for they do not allow one to state or think that he who is the preexistent Son of God the Father actually united himself in the womb, in these last days of the age, without confusion and without change, to flesh possessed of a rational soul, and that he thereby became one of us; instead, they insist on announcing, and also persuade people to agree, that God indwelt him as he would a saint. They fail to realize that, through the Spirit, the God of the universe is also within each of us, as in holy tem-

19. *Anthrôpotokos*, the term urged by Nestorius as an alternative to "Mother-of-God."

ples, as it says, "Do you not know that you are God's temple and God's Spirit lives in you? So if anyone ruins God's temple, God will ruin him; for the temple of God is holy, and that is what you are."[20] So if even we ourselves are called temples because God indwells us by his Spirit, then we can be sure that it is otherwise with the mystery of Christ. Now, given that we say that the flesh was genuinely united to God the Word, within whom was a rational soul, I would gladly learn of him whether he argues that the Word was genuinely united to the man, that is, to the rationally ensouled holy body; or whether he accords with others in thinking that it happened by a connection pertaining between a servant-like form without its own concrete existence and a divine form similarly without its own concrete existence; or in yet another way, by means of an ambiguity in the term "son" or by their sharing an equal dignity. It is really questionable whether one should entertain any such notion as "connection" anyway. Seeing as I am in possession of what that man has said and of his transparent confession, I am probably being unnecessarily upset about it and elaborating my defense more than is really necessary, for in his analysis of the first anathema, he says:

This is why we name the child who was born Emmanuel, who is neither God separated from human nature nor a man stripped of divinity.

Of course, he needed to explain this issue in an accurate and neatly-rounded way, but we must point out this one thing: see how, in this quotation, while obviously explaining the union, he says that God is not separated from the human nature, yet he also admits to knowing Christ to be one within the union, that is, that the same individual is at the same time both God and man. Surely he will be embarrassed at our critique?

ᖷ Second Anathema

If any do not confess that the Word from God the Father was united to flesh at the level of concrete existence, and that Christ is one, together with his own flesh, that is, that the same individual is at the same time both God and man, let them be anathema.

20. 1 Cor 3.16–17.

Theodoret's Critique

Because we are guided by the divine teachings of the apostles, we confess one Christ, and we call the same individual both God and man because they have been united. On the other hand, we do not recognize that the union was "at the level of concrete existence." Such a notion is wholly foreign both to the divine Scriptures and to the Fathers who have interpreted them. And if the author of this expression means by a union "at the level of concrete existence" that there arose a mixture of flesh and divinity, then we shall zealously oppose him and critique such a blasphemy. For confusion necessarily follows mixture, and once confusion has been introduced, then the property of each nature is removed. The elements of a mixture are no longer what they were before. This would be the most horrific of things to say about God the Word and of the one who came from David's seed. Rather, we should be convinced by the Lord when, by commanding the Jews to "destroy this temple and in three days I shall raise it up,"[21] he implied that there were two natures. If a mixture had arisen, then neither would God have remained God nor would the temple be recognized as a temple. Instead, the temple would have been by nature God and vice versa, since this is entailed by the definition of a mixture. In this case, it would have been superfluous for the Lord to command the Jews to "destroy this temple and in three days I shall raise it up." If some sort of mixture, and hence confusion, had really arisen, then he ought rather to have said, "Destroy me and in three days I shall be raised." But instead he implied that there were both a temple to be destroyed and a God who can raise it up again. Hence this "union at the level of concrete existence," which in my opinion is being offered to us as a cover for the term "mixture," is quite superfluous. It is sufficient to speak of "the union," a term which both implies the properties of the natures and also teaches us to worship a single Christ.

21. Jn 2.19.

Cyril's Defense

See again what a noble chap he is! He takes whatever chance he can to natter on against me, so keen is he to rip apart this expression of mine, "at the level of concrete existence." He condemns it for not being a customary term and asserts that it is a strange, made-up expression. He does not appreciate that the meaning of these words is being deployed to defend the truth against the new-fangled words of profane heretics, and he attempts to do away with what seems to be the opposition.

It is precisely because Nestorius constantly denied that God the Word's birth happened according to flesh, and instead introduced a mere unity of dignities, and it is because he said that a man, honored by sharing the title of Sonship, was connected to God, that we were forced to battle against these notions of his and to assert instead that the union was "at the level of concrete existence," meaning by this simply that the Word's nature, that is, his concrete existence, which is the Word himself, was genuinely united to a human nature, quite apart from any change or confusion, as we have said often enough. He is reckoned to be, and actually is, a single Christ; the same individual is both God and man.

I do think that Theodoret would actually agree on this point, since he says that the god is not separated from human nature nor is the humanity reckoned apart from divinity. We do not agree, however, that the forms, the servant's and God's, were united apart from their concrete existences, nor would we affirm that a regular man was honored by a mere equality of dignities and was contingently connected to the Word. What we do say is that the Only-Begotten Son of God himself took upon himself the flesh possessed of a rational soul that had been united to him and became a man while remaining also God. But this man, who is so smart with his words and has such a keen intelligence, argues that the expression implies mixture, and he even dares to suggest that the integrity of the natures would be damaged by being part of this mixture, as if we did not know this.

See how he goes on and on and loves the sound of his own

words. He reckons he has no equal in speaking at great length, and he accepts something that has never been said before as if it were the truth, such that he seems to be one of those people who do not know how to discern right from wrong, one of whom might make up deceitful stories while another might straightway find the right path and make use of sensible and appropriate expressions. I confess that at first I believed that he understood the meaning of the anathemas and that he was just pretending not to, so as to indulge certain individuals. But I now realize that actually he does not have a clue.

ᗱ *Third Anathema*

If any divide the concrete existences of the one Christ after the union, connecting them by a connection that is merely one of dignity, authority, or power, rather than by a convergence at the level of a natural union, let them be anathema.

Theodoret's Critique

The meanings of his expressions are totally unclear, even opaque, though for godly people it is clear that they are meaningless, since is there anyone who cannot see that "connection" and "convergence" mean just the same thing? Convergence is something that happens to things that are separate, while connection is something that happens to things that are divided. The extremely cunning author of these expressions has turned synonyms into opposites. He says that we must not speak of a "connection" by which the concrete existences become attached to one another,[22] but rather of a "convergence," and a natural one at that. Either he does not know what he is talking about, or else he is consciously being blasphemous. You see, nature has to do with what is involuntary, what is inevitable; for example, we say that we hunger naturally, meaning that we do not decide to be hungry; it happens inevitably. If they were able to will not to be hungry, then paupers would surely have stopped begging! Being thirsty, sleeping, and breathing the air are all things done

22. Lit.: "connected."

naturally; as I have said, they are all examples of things that are involuntary. Any who do not feel the need of such things must be at the end of their lives. So if the union of God's form with the form of the servant had been a natural one, then God the Word would have been forced by necessity to be connected to the form of the servant, instead of its being something given out of his love of humanity, and he who gave laws to the whole world would turn out to be the one who is constrained to follow those laws. That is not what the blessed Paul taught us; on the contrary, he said that "he emptied himself, taking the form of a servant."[23] The phrase "he emptied himself" implies that it was done voluntarily. So then, if he was consciously and deliberately united to the human nature that he took, then it is superfluous to add this qualification, "natural," it being quite enough to acknowledge that there was a union, a union moreover that pertains to things previously divided, since without there being some division between things, a union would not be conceivable. So, the supposition of a union presupposes a division. And if so, how can he say that one cannot divide the concrete existences or natures? Especially as he knows full well both that the concrete existence of God the Word was complete even before time began, and that the servant's form he took was also a complete form. This is why he said "concrete existences" and not "concrete existence." Given, then, that the natures, that is, God's form and the servant's form, the one that was taken, are both complete things that nonetheless came together into the same individual, it is reasonable to acknowledge a single person and, of course, a single Son and Christ, while to refer to the "united concrete existences," or natures, is not inappropriate but is actually a necessary consequence. For if in the case of a single human being we divide the natures and call the mortal one "body" and the immortal one "soul," but both together are called "man," it is even more reasonable to recognize the properties of both the natures: that of God, who takes, and that of the man, who is taken. We find even the blessed Paul dividing a single man into two when he said somewhere, "As much as our external self wastes away, so much is our internal self re-

23. Phil 2.7.

newed";[24] then elsewhere, "It is in the inner self that I rejoice
in God's law";[25] and again, "that Christ may dwell in the inner
self."[26] Hence, if even the Apostle divides the natural connection between natures that exist contemporaneously, how can
this man, whose doctrine is really one of mixture (though without using that term) indict us of impiety for dividing the properties of the two natures, namely, the nature of the eternal God
and the nature of the man who was taken up in these last days?

Cyril's Defense

This man who seems to know everything considers first of
all that the obscurity of what I say is deceitful, and also that this
perfectly clear and well-known term (at least it is to anyone who
cares to think straight) is totally opaque. He is the one whose
mind's eye is darkened. He thought that the argument we prof-
fered demanded that one use the term "convergence" and not
the term "connection," and then, as a way of demonstrating his
inner deviousness, he makes out that the meaning is the same
whether one uses the term "connection" or the term "convergence." I was quite surprised that he showed such poor judgment in this matter, for apparently *he* is the only one who knows
what absolutely everybody knows, something so clichéd that it is
blatantly obvious to anyone who tries to avoid worldly thinking,
rhetorical word games, or science based on vague hearsay. It is
because I am so in awe of his wide learning, that I say this: you,
with your mouth gaping so widely against us, wake up a bit from
your drunken sleep, and look more minutely into the mystery.
There are some who slander this so-called union that concerns
Christ, and in opposition to what it says in Holy Scripture they
twist it into something perverted, whatever they happen to feel
like. For example, they say that the natures are totally divided
from one another, that they are separate in every way, and that
each has its own separate existence; they hold that the man was
contingently connected to God merely at the level of dignity
or authority, and because the word "son" can be predicated of

24. 2 Cor 4.16.   25. Rom 7.22.
26. Eph 3.16–17.

both of them.[27] The anathema does away with this doctrine and takes a stand against such nauseating and meaningless stuff. We maintain that the Word was naturally, that is, genuinely, not contingently, united to the holy flesh, which possessed a rational soul. We do not need to split it up in any way, lest we end up thinking of two sons because we have divided the indivisible. But he fails to comprehend what this "natural union" means, namely, that it is genuine, one that neither confuses nor mixes the natures together such that each would need to be in a different state from what it actually is. He uses a juvenile and silly explanation as proof of what he reckons to be right and says,

If the union was a natural one, then the Word's self-emptying was not something voluntary, but such as would arise from necessity and constraint, since nature has to do with what is involuntary.

Against this, one might reply to him that, yes, as you say, hunger, thirst, etc., are natural infirmities of the flesh and affect us because we have natures that are subject to the affections, but the Word's divine and ineffable nature admits neither of affection nor of necessity and is in no way constrained such that it would be required, against its will, to become flesh, that is, to make a limited humanity its own and take upon itself Abraham's seed.[28]

It is easy for anyone who wants to, to see that this argument is totally futile. He states that things that are natural are in every way subject to the laws of necessity, adducing as proof of this the fact that we experience hunger and thirst involuntarily, since nature calls even when we do not want it to. But a learned man, one who has a mind sharply attuned towards such matters, ought to see that there are other issues here that should rightly be taken more into account. After all, is it not true that man is naturally rational? Is the rational involuntary and constrained? What next? Tell me also, whether the God of the universe is not naturally God? Is he not naturally holy, just, good, life, light, wisdom, and power? Is he what he is against his will, by necessity,

27. Cyril uses the term "homonymy" in the Aristotelian sense, drawn from the opening chapter of the *Categories*.

28. Cf. Heb 2.16.

as it were? To think along such lines is the very limit of madness and would, I reckon, be worthy of a transparent rebuttal. Why does he try to turn his deceit into some sort of unassailable bastion and grasp at such a feeble defense? Then, when he hears us say that the union is natural, that is, that it is genuine and free from change and that the convergence of the concrete existences is altogether unconfused, he tries to twist the meaning of what I say so that it would seem to have been wrongly expressed. The brazen man is not afraid to make the Word's nature submit to inescapable necessity and thereby make him like us. It was not an involuntary act when he emptied himself. The Only-Begotten voluntarily became a man; it was not as you say, that he took a man to himself, bestowing this connection upon himself contingently and crowning himself with the grace that sonship entails, as could happen in the case of a human being. The result is that we believe the concrete existences to have been united and the Word to have become man and incarnate, and hence we appropriately refer to the union as "natural." It is a doctrine of the union that excludes its being counterfeit or contingent (and it is something we possess by faith and sanctification, because we have become partakers of the divine nature, as Paul says, "he that is joined to the Lord is one spirit"),[29] and which does not subject the Word of God, who is free and without affection, to constraints and natural desires. It seems to me that one cannot reproach or upbraid this desire not to separate after the union what has been joined or to push them apart from each other, especially when that lovely chap Theodoret takes as an example a human being, which in our view would be a single entity, and does not allow him to be split up, albeit he does admit that there is some such split or separation in our perception of a human being—I mean to the extent that one knows that the soul and the flesh are in their own natures quite different things. If we now take this latter point into account in considering the mode of the union that occurred in Christ, then we would conclude that, as an object of our intellection, there was a genuine convergence between divinity and humanity into a union, although we know full well that the Word of

29. 1 Cor 6.17.

God in his own nature is something quite different from the flesh while the latter is also a different entity in *its* own nature. Once they have been united, though, it is dangerous to split them up again, while orthodox logic, as the holy and divinely inspired Scriptures teach us, does not allow anyone to partition the one Christ, Son, and Lord into two Sons. *His* treatment, however, of these questions of true doctrine is altogether superficial. In fact, he spurns any knowledge that would be vital for him to do this to advantage, as if this were something harmful. Instead, he appears to glory in his deceit even when he is made well aware of his slanders; let him hear what we have to say: "Why do you, strong man, boast of wrongdoing in your evil? All day your tongue has plotted unrighteousness."[30]

৯৶ Fourth Anathema

If any allocate the sayings in the evangelical and apostolic writings to two persons, or concrete existences, whether those spoken by the saints about Christ or those he used about himself, and then attribute some of them to a man who is thought of separately from the Word of God, and others only to the Word of God because they are more appropriate to God, let them be anathema.

Theodoret's Refutation

This statement is similar to the previous ones. Given that there has been a mixture, he proposes that there is no distinction to be made among the sayings in the holy Gospels or in the apostolic writings, and he boasts that he can still meanwhile resist Arianism, Eunomianism, and other such heresies.[31] So let this great teacher of theology explain how he would refute these heretics' blasphemies by attributing the more inferior sayings, those more appropriately spoken by the form of the servant, to God the Word. Those heretics make out that God the

---

30. Ps 52.1–2 (51.3–4 LXX).
31. For the significance of this accusation for Cyril's future and his experience at the Council of Ephesus, see Introduction, pp. 19–20.

Word is a lesser entity, a creature and servant, and they teach that the Son of God came into existence from non-existence. So as for us who hold the opposite position, who confess the Son to be consubstantial and co-eternal with God the Father, who say that the Son is the Maker of all, the one who creates, orders, governs, rules, who is all-wise and all-powerful (more, that he is power itself, life itself, wisdom itself), to whom should we attribute the saying, "My God, my God, why have you forsaken me?" or, "Father, if possible, let this cup pass from me," or, "Father, save me from this hour," or, "No one knows that hour, not even the Son of Man,"[32] and all other such humble sayings that he himself uttered, or that the holy apostles said or wrote about him? To whom should we attribute the hunger and the thirst, the tiredness and the sleep, the ignorance and the fear? Who was it who needed the help of angels? If the answer is God the Word, then how could it be that Wisdom was ignorant? And could someone afflicted by ignorance be called "Wisdom"? If he did not have the Father's knowledge, how could he have been speaking the truth when he said that he himself had everything the Father had?[33] After all, he said, "Only the Father knows that day."[34] How could he be the perfect image of his Begetter without possessing all that belonged to the Begetter? If someone admits to being ignorant, and they are being truthful, that would be generally accepted, but if someone knows the day but desires to conceal it, and for that reason pretends ignorance, then the result is quite some blasphemy indeed! Either the truth is lying, or else it cannot really be called the truth because it contains something of the opposite. Yet if the truth does not lie, then God the Word knew full well about that day which in fact he himself created and which he himself appointed as the day on which he intends to judge the world. Since he is the Father's perfect image, he has the Father's knowledge. Hence it was not God the Word who was lacking in this knowledge; it was the form of the servant, which at that exact time knew only as much as the indwelling Godhead had revealed to him. The same can

32. Mt 27.46; Mt 26.39; Jn 12.27; Mt 24.36.
33. Cf. Jn 16.15.
34. Mt 24.36.

be said also about other similar passages. Otherwise, how could God the Word reasonably say to the Father, "Father, if possible, let this cup pass from me; nevertheless, not as I will but as you will"?[35] Again, all sorts of absurd consequences follow, such as that the Father and the Son are not of one mind—the Father wants one thing, the Son another, as he says, "nevertheless, not as I will but as you will." We note that yet again the Son turns out to be very ignorant since he does not know whether or not the cup will pass from him. But surely to say such a thing about God the Word is extremely blasphemous. He who came for this very purpose, who willingly took up into himself our nature and emptied himself, he knew precisely what the end result of the mysterious plan of salvation was. This is why he could predict to the holy apostles what would happen: "Look, we are going up to Jerusalem, and the Son of Man shall be given into the clutches of the Gentiles for them to mock him, flog him, and crucify him; on the third day he will rise again."[36] So, how can he pray against all this happening when he knew the whole future and had predicted it and even rebuked Peter for praying that it would not happen? It is totally absurd for Abraham to have seen his day long ago and to have rejoiced,[37] and for Isaiah similarly to have prophesied about his saving passion (not to mention Jeremiah, Daniel, Zechariah, and the whole gamut of the prophets), while all the time he is ignorant, pleads for an escape, and prays that what was going to happen for the sake of world salvation would not come to pass. Surely, then, it was not God the Word who said these things; it was the form of the servant, fearful of a death that had not yet been destroyed. God the Word permitted it to say such things, granting an opportunity for it to show fear so as to reveal clearly the nature of the element that had been received and so that we would not take him who was from Abraham and David for an appearance or fantasy. This docetic blasphemy arose precisely because that irreligious, heretical lot chased after such ideas. To conclude, then, we shall attribute to God the Word everything that was said or done in a manner worthy of God, while whatever was

35. Mt 26.39.
37. Cf. Jn 8.56.

36. Cf. Mt 20.18–19.

said or done in a more inferior manner we shall assign to the form of the servant. This way we avoid being infected with the blasphemies of Arianism and Eunomianism.

Cyril's Defense

Would it not be so much better, my esteemed colleague, to launch this inquiry into the meanings of these terms without prejudice or an antagonistic attitude? But he does not do this at all; instead, he keeps coming back to what he feels like, and says:

> This statement is similar to the previous ones. Given that there has been a mixture, he proposes that there is no distinction to be made among the sayings in the holy Gospels or in the apostolic writings, and he boasts that he can still meanwhile resist Arianism, Eunomianism, and other such heresies.

That is what *he* says, but in fact I am as far from suggesting that the natures are mixed with one another or that they undergo combination, confusion, or change, as he is from getting anything right at all! Moreover, we never denied that a distinction does need to be made between different sayings; we are aware that some of them are more appropriate to the divine, others to the human; the former belong to transcendent glory, while the latter fit better with the limitations of his emptying of himself. What we are saying is that there is absolutely no need to distribute them between two persons that are in any way at all separated from each other. For if our Lord Jesus Christ is one, and one the faith we have in him, and one the baptism, then one also surely is his person; that is, it is of a single individual. If the same individual is at the same time both God and man, then there can be no risk in making the sayings, both those appropriate to divinity and especially those appropriate to humanity, equally applicable to that individual. His deity and ineffable nature is in no way impoverished in comparison with the Father's transcendence just because he says something that is typically human; and neither is our faith in the saving effects of the Incarnation removed when it is proclaimed that along with being God he has also become a man like us. So whether a saying is appropriate to the divinity or is something human, in both cases it belongs to the single Christ. If the Word of God the Father did not become a man, then do not let him talk as one of us. But if it is true that he "partook of blood and flesh alongside us" and "became like his brothers" (meaning us) "in every way,"[38] then why is it that they so mindlessly ridicule the wonderfully conceived plan of salvation by not making any allowance for things said on the human level or for that lowliness of speech which is entailed by the means of salvation, just because, as they readily admit, they are desperate to keep the Son on his own, separate from the form of the servant? It is quite mad to pretend to be afraid of the perversions of heretics and then to end up removing the orthodox tradition right out of its proper definition. It would be better, and certainly more intelligible, to say that the human sayings are not to be attributed to a different person (or rather, a son conceived of separately and on his own account), to the form of the servant, as they would usually have it, but instead to attribute them to his human limitations. For it was inevitable, if he was at the same time both God and man, that he would make use of both types of sayings. What amazes me is how hypocritical he can be in confessing that Christ is one, that is, that the same individual is at the same time both God and man, and then divide the one into two, as if he had drifted off into forgetting what he had previously taken to be correct. For he quotes the Savior's saying, "Nobody knows about that day or that hour, not even the heavenly angels, nor the Son, but only the Father,"[39] and then, while affirming that the Word begotten of God the Father is Wisdom itself and knows the whole future, he goes on to say,

[I]t was not God the Word who was lacking in this knowledge; it was the form of the servant, which at that exact time knew only as much as the indwelling Godhead had revealed to him. The same can be said also about the other similar passages.

So if you are not lying when you call Jesus one Christ and Lord and say that the same individual is at the same time both

38. Heb 2.14, 17.
39. Mt 24.36.

God and man, why do you then divide him, and why are you not embarrassed to mention two sons? If the one who is omniscient is not identical with the one who has limited knowledge—the one perfect in wisdom, who knows all that the Father knows, not identical with the one who receives only a partial revelation—then certainly there would indeed be two subjects. And if because of the fact of there being a genuine union he is actually one and the same individual, not two separate things, each on its own, then knowing and also not knowing can both be reasonably predicated of him. He has divine knowledge because he is the Father's wisdom, but since for salvation's sake he has subjected himself to the boundaries of human knowledge, then this boundary he has made his very own along with the other characteristics, even though, as I just mentioned, there is nothing he does not know—in fact, he has complete knowledge like the Father. What is the reason, then, that one may say that he was hungry or that he was travel-weary,[40] even though he is Life and, as God, the Giver of life, and also the living Bread come down from heaven who gives life to the world,[41] and who is himself likened to the Lord of powers?[42] Well, so that we might believe that he really did become a man, he made the human characteristics his very own, albeit continuing to enjoy the full possession of his own nature's virtues, retaining without confusion the state in which he was, is, and ever shall be. Arguing that God indwelt the form of the servant and granted him a revelation, and that a partial one, suggests to us that Emmanuel is merely a prophet and a god-bearing man, and nothing else. He reckons that to be sensible and uncontroversial. If (following his argument) it was the Word of God who cried, "Father, if possible, let this cup pass from me,"[43] then in the first place he is not of one mind with the Father, and, further, he is wrong to pray against drinking the cup, even though he knows full well that his Passion is going to be for the world's salvation. He infers, then, that these sayings were not made by God the Word. Therefore, anyone who goes along with such spurious arguments will get some comeback from us. Since you think that such sayings ought to come

40. Jn 4.6.
42. Cf. Ps 24(23):10.

41. Jn 6.51, 33.
43. Mt 26.39.

nowhere near God the Word and that they should be attributed only to the form of the servant, are you not thereby dividing
the one back again into two sons? So much is obvious to anyone
with half a mind! After all, even someone who follows your line
of reasoning, my friend, would agree that there is absolutely no
way that the form of the servant would pray against the Passion
or would appear to have a different intention from the Father
and even from the indwelling Logos himself. Surely, I might
suggest, he knew that the Passion was going to bring salvation
to everything under heaven and give life to those defeated by
death. He then goes on to say that he had to be seen to be above
cowardice and always to be following divine prompting. Do you
not realize that you are nattering on pointlessly? What a pile of
disgusting garbage these ideas of yours are! Without a moment's
hesitation I would say that all human characteristics are of little
worth next to the Word that was begotten of God. Moreover, I
will ask him, to whom do you think the self-emptying happened,
and who would be the one who willingly underwent it? If you
reply, as some do, that it was the form of the servant, namely,
David's seed, then how could that possibly be emptied, if he was
taken up by God? And if you say that it was the very Word himself, who is formally equal to God the Father, who emptied himself, then again how could he possibly be emptied if he avoided
the self-emptying? No, for God the Word, who has no knowledge
or experience of change, to empty himself means precisely to
do and to say something characteristically human, on account of
his saving convergence with flesh. Of course, even though he became a man, the logic of this mysterious process absolutely does
not imply that any damage would have been done to his own
nature. He both remained what he was and also came down into
humanity for the salvation and life of the world. That is why we
attribute his sayings, both those in the Gospels and those in the
writings of the holy apostles, not to two persons but to a single
Christ, Son, and God. Neither do we allow his human characteristics to belittle his divine nature and glory, nor do we disown the
plan of salvation. Rather, we believe that the Incarnation that
was for our sakes is to be predicated of the Word himself.

🕭 Fifth Anathema

If any dare to say that Christ is a god-bearing man and not rather that he is truly God because he is by nature the one natural Son, insofar as the Word became flesh and "partook like us of blood and flesh,"[44] let them be anathema.

Theodoret's Critique

We agree that, insofar as he was united to blood, flesh, and immortal soul, God the Word partook of such things just as we do. At the same time, though, we wholly deny that he was made flesh by any sort of change and even charge with profanity anyone who says so. In fact, this turns out to be the very opposite to what the verse actually means. For if the Word was changed into flesh, then he cannot have partaken with us of flesh and blood, while if he partook of flesh and blood, then he did so because he was something different from flesh and blood. Hence, if the flesh is something different from him, then he cannot himself have changed into flesh. This is why, by using the expression "partaking," we worship as a single Son both him who took and that which was taken, and at the same time acknowledge that their natures are different. And no, we do not reject the term "god-bearing man" since it may be found in many of the holy Fathers, including Basil the Great, who uses this term as a name in his *To Amphilochius, On the Holy Spirit,* and also in his exegesis of Psalm 59.[45] It is not because he was only partially in receipt of divine grace that we bestow this title upon him, but because he possessed the entire united deity of the Son. For this is how the blessed Paul interpreted it: "Take care that no one snare you

44. Heb 2.14.

45. *On the Holy Spirit* 5.12; also at *Homilies on the Psalms* 59.58 (PG 29:468B), an important citation for Theodoret in the florilegium he included in his *Eranistes.* In both cases (and in the small number of other occurrences in Basil) the term actually is predicated of "flesh" rather than of "man." The term "god-bearing man" was often used of prophets and saints (e.g., in Chrysostom's eulogy of Ignatius); hence Cyril's understandable reticence to use it of God the Word.

with philosophy and empty deceit, which comes from human tradition and is based on the elements of this world rather than on Christ, because the whole fullness of divinity dwells bodily in him."[46]

Cyril's Defense

Yet again it is easy to prove that he is spouting garbage. What I am asserting is that it is inappropriate for anyone to call Christ a god-bearing man, the aim being to ensure that he is reckoned to be God genuinely made man, the Word of God incarnate, not just like some saint. But yet again this fellow is launching his attack against perfectly orthodox statements and indulging in all sorts of extraordinary deceits. For instance, he says that my argument is that the Word of God was transformed into the flesh's nature, and so he goes digging round for arguments to prove how the Word of God could never be changeable. So I have to say yet again what I have already said so often, namely, that since no one is suggesting that the Word's divine and pure nature was transformed into earthly flesh, and everyone agrees that his nature is unchangeable, it is a total waste of effort to feel obliged to deal with such fraudulent claims that arise from nothing, because God the Word is naturally unchangeable and unalterable. After all, who would be so utterly senseless as willfully to think or say such shocking things that even the most mindless idiot would throw out with the trash? I am quite taken aback that there is such a person who attributes to the Emmanuel the limitations of being a prophet, even when it is universally agreed by everyone that Emmanuel is God. He actually calls him a god-bearing man, in which case he would seem to be just like us insofar as, by means of the Holy Spirit, we have the God of the universe dwelling within us; he lives in our hearts, and "we are temples of the living God."[47] To think that God lived in a man is not the same thing as to say that the Word became a man. If what the blessed Paul said is true, that the whole fullness of the Godhead was pleased to dwell in him bodily (that

46. Col 2.8–9.
47. Cf. 1 Cor 3.16–17; 2 Cor 6.16.

is, not contingently),[48] then he is telling us that God the Father is one, and that the Lord Jesus Christ, through whom are all things, is also one. One might say that a man's spirit lives within him (and that is why Scripture says that "as for those who dwell in houses of clay, among whom we also are formed of the same clay"),[49] but a man is nonetheless reckoned to be single, and indeed is really so because he is a composition of his flesh and the rational soul that dwells within him. So why can he not stop muddling up my straightforward and accurate explanation of the doctrine? One moment he is saying there is a single Christ, Son, and Lord, the same individual who is at once both God and man; then at another he surrenders him to the limitations of the prophets by calling him a god-bearing man. Is he so unaware that, if he is a temple indwelt by the Word just as we are, rather than genuinely being God, then that makes him basically equivalent to us? Yet that is not how the divinely inspired Scriptures have it ("the Word became flesh and made his dwelling among us").[50] It was said this way precisely so that no one might think that he had been transformed into the nature of flesh by any sort of change. The one who became flesh, that is, man, is not a god-bearing man. He is God. He descended willingly into his state of self-emptying and made the flesh from a woman his very own, flesh that has both soul and mind. Remember that he calls his own body a temple,[51] though this indwelling was not contingent as it is when the Spirit indwells us. Rather, because they have been united, he is reckoned as a single Christ, Son, and Lord.

ʒ❦ *Sixth Anathema*

If any say that the Word of God the Father is the God or Lord of Christ, and do not instead acknowledge that the same individual is at the same time both God and man, since the Scriptures say that the Word became flesh, let them be anathema.

---

48. Cf. Col 1.19; 2.9.   49. Jb 4.19.
50. Jn 1.14.   51. Cf. Jn 2.19.

Theodoret's Critique

The blessed Paul names what was taken up by God the Word as the "form of a servant."[52] Since, however, this "taking-up" happened before the union and since the blessed Paul was discussing the "taking-up" when he called the nature that was taken the "form of a servant," then the reference to a "servant" no longer applies after the union has occurred. If he was writing to people who believed in Christ when the Apostle said, "so you are no longer a servant but a son,"[53] and if the Lord said to his disciples, "I shall no longer call you servants but friends,"[54] then how much more is he who is the first-fruits of our nature, he by whom we were made worthy of the grace of adoption, made free from the name of "servant." So we agree that even the "form of the servant" is God because God's form was united with it, and we have no problem with the prophet calling even the infant Emmanuel and naming the child who was born a "messenger of great counsel," and a "wonderful counsellor, mighty and powerful God, Prince of peace, and Father of eternity."[55] Even so, even after the union the very same prophet proclaimed the nature of what was taken and called the one from Abraham's seed a "servant," as in these sayings: "You are my servant, Israel, and in you shall I be glorified," and, "Thus says the Lord, who formed me from the womb as his servant," and a little later, "Behold, I have given you as a covenant for nations, for a light to Gentiles, that you may be a salvation right to the end of the earth."[56] So what was formed in the womb was not God the Word but the form of the servant, since God the Word did not become flesh by being changed. He took up to himself flesh possessing a rational soul.

52. Phil 2.7.   53. Gal 4.7.

54. Jn 15.15.

55. Is 7.14; 9.6. The latter of these verses was known to Theodoret according to the Lucianic recension, in which the Hebrew names had been restored to a much truncated LXX text. Theodoret discusses these issues in his commentary on Isaiah, written within a few years of this controversy, where it is used to similar purpose; see *Commentaire sur Isaïe,* ed. J.-N. Guinot, Sources chrétiennes 276, vol. 1 (Paris: Éditions du Cerf, 1980), 326–27.

56. Is 49.3–6.

Cyril's Defense

The mystery of salvation brought about by the Incarnation of the Only-Begotten easily proves that the formula that we constructed, and that he is now defending just as much, was entirely appropriate. For he who exists in the form of God the Father is the Only-Begotten Son. He is on a par with his Father in every possible way. He shares the same glory and freedom, and yet he took upon himself the form of a servant and was called a brother to those who are under the yoke of slavery, namely, us.[57] Moreover, although he was the Lawmaker insofar as he was God, he paid his tax to the tax-collectors like one of us and became like a man under the law; yet he taught his disciples that actually he was the Son, and that, as a result of his Incarnation, he was in the form of a servant, while in his own nature he remained free since he was from God, and was God. He bore with the tax-gatherers only because, by possessing the form of the servant as his very own, his self-emptying had limited that freedom. One ought not, as a result, to be offended if someone calls him a "servant" after the usage of the holy prophets, since they were aware, because the Holy Spirit revealed it to them, both that, once the Word of God the Father had become a man, he would be free insofar as he is the Son, but also that, by sharing a form with us who are under the yoke of slavery, his limitations (which were all part of the grand design of his self-emptying) would not put him in contempt. That is why he can say that God is his Father, even though he is God by nature and came out of him, and even though his transcendence is in no way less than his Father's. Now, Nestorius wrote of Christ as follows: "that he who suffers is a merciful high priest, not the life-giving God of him who suffered," and he also calls the Word of God "the God of Christ"; and even though he adds that "the child and the child's master are one and the same," we still insist that these expressions of his are not only misplaced but positively blasphemous. For if the Word of God the Father is "the God of Christ," there would clearly and indisputably be two individuals; so how could the child and the child's master then be reckoned to be one and the same? If it is the case that the

57. Cf. Gal 5.1.

same individual is at the same time both God and man, because the Word of God has been made man and incarnate, then you could not say that Emmanuel was the God and master of himself. How could anyone possibly think that way, when we all know that divinity, within the context of its own nature, is something quite different from humanity in the context of *its* own nature? Christ, though, is one individual comprised from both divinity and humanity, and this in the context of the union that brings salvation.

⁊❧ *Seventh Anathema*

If any say that Jesus's actions were carried out by God the Word as a man's would be,[58] and that he was endowed with the glory of the Only-Begotten as if he were another individual with a separate existence, let them be anathema.

Theodoret's Critique

If it is human nature to be mortal, while God the Word is Life and the Life-giver, who raised up the temple that had been destroyed by the Jews and took it up to heaven, then surely the form of the servant has been glorified through the form of God. If the form of the servant started by being naturally mortal and then became immortal by being united to God the Word, then it received what it did not have; it is because it took what it did not have and was thus glorified that the form of the servant has been glorified by the Giver. That is why the Apostle exclaims, "according to the working of his mighty power which he accomplished in Christ when he raised him from the dead."[59]

Cyril's Defense

Those who refer to Christ as the Word of God rather than as a man just like us are demonstrating thereby, to anyone who

---

58. *Energeô:* This verb is used by Cyril both directly of Jesus and of his activities. A more accurate translation of the anathema might be, "if anyone says that Jesus was controlled by God the Word," but the English "carried out" allows the term to be translated the same way throughout this passage, which is preferable.

59. Eph 1.19–20.

will listen, that he was made man and incarnate. Hence, even if anything that is especially appropriate to the divinity were said to have been carried out through his body, which was thereby fulfilling the function of an instrument in his hands, it would be no less the case that the one carrying out the action was the Lord of powers, who was not granting that power of control to someone else in the way that he granted authority to the blessed apostles over "unclean spirits, to cast them out and heal every disease and every deformity among the people."[60] The divinely inspired Paul also says, "I will not dare to talk about anything but what Christ has carried out through me, by both word and deed, through signs and wonders, in the power of the Holy Spirit."[61] The blessed disciples rejoiced and later approached Christ and said, "Lord, even the demons obeyed us in your name."[62] For we argue that, through the Spirit, Christ carried out the actions of the saints, who were separate individuals, but we do not think that the Word carried out the actions of Jesus through the Spirit in this way, as if he were a separate son beside God's Only-Begotten. The notion of the union implies singularity, and hence we take care not to make a division into two. Even when the Scriptures say that the Word became flesh, he is also the Only-Begotten Son because there was a genuine, albeit impossible to express or understand, union between them. That is precisely why we argue that the one and only Christ Jesus carried out the miracles using his very own body as an instrument and that this did not happen in the same way as in the case of the saints; such a parallel would be wholly profane and unacceptable. If, however, it was his very own body that he raised from the dead (because he is both Life and the Life-giver), then he would seem to be glorifying himself and showing how his own nature is life-giving rather than granting some other individual his own glory. Admittedly, even though he is God, comes naturally out of God, and is Lord of glory, he did say to God the Father in heaven, "Father, glorify me with the glory which I had with you before the world existed,"[63] in which case how can it be that he asks for the glory he had before the world began as if he

60. Mt 10.1.   61. Rom 15.18–19.
62. Lk 10.17.   63. Jn 17.5.

now lacked it? For since he became a man and by God's grace tasted death in his own flesh for everyone, as the blessed Paul says,[64] he avoided the ignominy of lacking glory by predicting his own resurrection, by which he would be recognized as both Life and Life-giver (because he is God), and thus would cause us to believe in him. He therefore glorified not some other individual but himself and demonstrated that the temple that had genuinely been united to him was above death. After all, we have said again and again that we believe that the body united to him was possessed of both soul and mind.

૨ Eighth Anathema

If any dare to say that the man who was taken up should be worshiped, glorified, and named together with God the Word, as if they were two separate individuals (for the addition of the term "together with" would always entail this understanding), rather than honoring Emmanuel with a single act of worship and ascribing to him a single act of praise, seeing that the Word became flesh, let them be anathema.

Theodoret's Critique

As I have said often enough, we offer a single act of praise to our master Christ, and we acknowledge that the same individual is at the same time both God and man, since the definition of union requires this. But this does not mean that we have to avoid talking about the special properties of each of the natures. God the Word did not undergo any change into flesh, nor did the man cease to be what he was and transform into the nature of God. Hence we still refer to the properties of each nature even while we are worshiping Christ our Master.

Cyril's Defense

But then we, my dear friend, are used to having far better and more accurate explanations. We follow more detailed lines

---

64. Cf. Heb 2.9.

of reasoning in trying to unpack the mystery and gain an insight into it that is both precise and is also in line with the teachings of Holy Scripture and the reasoning of the holy Fathers. Hence we deny that God the Word took up for himself a man or connected himself with a man in some contingent fashion as if purely external. We specify that he became a man, and for this very reason we assert that anyone who dares suggest that we need to speak of a man being "taken up" or that we should worship him together with the Son of God, as if they were separate individuals, has departed from orthodox doctrine. For if the same individual is at the same time both God and man, then he is to be worshiped as one individual with a single act of worship, not worshiped "together with" God, or named "together with" God. Otherwise, we might be led to believe in Emmanuel as just a man like one of us who shares in the divine glory, only by grace. No, he is to be acknowledged as God, made flesh for our sakes, that is, genuinely made man, not because his nature was transformed by any sort of change, but because that was the plan of salvation achieved by the union.

ঽ Ninth Anathema

If any suggest that the one Lord Jesus Christ was glorified by the Spirit by making use of a power that came through the Spirit, a power that was something other than his own, and that he received from the Spirit the ability to overcome evil spirits and perform divine miracles for people, instead of saying that the Spirit by which he wrought the miracles was his very own, let them be anathema.

Theodoret's Critique

On this occasion he has dared openly to anathematize not just godly people in the present day, but also those who proclaimed the truth in former ages, and even the authors of the divine Gospels, the band of holy apostles, and above all the archangel Gabriel himself. For he was the very first who, even before the conception, proclaimed that Christ would be born in the flesh from the Holy Spirit, and said the same to Joseph after the conception. To Mary, when she asked, "How can this happen to me, since I have not known a man?" he replied, "The Holy Spirit will come upon you, and the power of the Most High will overshadow you; for this reason what is born is holy and shall be called Son of God."[65] He also said to Joseph, "Do not fear to take Mary your wife, for what she is bearing is from the Holy Spirit."[66] The evangelist also comments, "When his mother Mary had been betrothed to Joseph, she was found to be with child from the Holy Spirit."[67] Even the Lord himself, upon entering the synagogue of the Jews and taking up the prophet Isaiah, read the passage that says, "The Spirit of the Lord is upon me, because he has anointed me," etc., and then added, "Today this Scripture has been fulfilled in your hearing."[68] The blessed Peter discussed the same topic with the Jews: "Jesus of Nazareth, whom God anointed with the Holy Spirit."[69] Isaiah had predicted these very events many generations earlier: "A rod will come forth out of the stem of Jesse, and a flower shall emerge from the root, and God's Spirit shall rest upon him, the spirit of wisdom and of understanding, the spirit of counsel and of strength, the spirit of knowledge and of godliness; he shall be filled with a spirit that fears God."[70] And also, "Behold, my servant whom I have chosen, my beloved, in whom my soul has rejoiced. I shall set my spirit upon him; he shall bring judgment upon the Gentiles."[71] The evangelist also cited this testimony in his own accounts,[72] and even the Lord himself declared to the Jews in the Gospels, "If it is by God's Spirit that I cast out the demons, then God's kingdom has surely come upon you."[73] John, too, said that "he who sent me to baptize with water told me himself, 'The one on whom you see the Spirit coming down and resting, he is the one who baptizes with the Holy Spirit.'"[74]

65. Lk 1.34–35.
66. Mt 1.20.
67. Mt 1.18.
68. Lk 4.16–21.
69. Acts 10.38.

70. Is 11.1–2. In his commentary on Isaiah, Theodoret again uses this verse to underline the fleshly ancestry of the Messiah.

71. Is 42.1.
72. Mt 3.17.
73. Mt 12.28.
74. Jn 1.33.

So, then, this exacting auditor of godly doctrine has anathematized not merely prophets and apostles, nor even just the archangel Gabriel, but has extended the blasphemy even to the Savior of all himself. After all, we have already shown that it was the Lord himself who read the words, "The Spirit of the Lord is upon me, because he has anointed me," and then said to the Jews, "Today this Scripture has been fulfilled in your ears," and who also said to those who charged him with casting out demons by Beelzebub that he was in fact casting them out by God's Spirit. Nonetheless, we deny that he who was formed by the Holy Spirit and anointed by it was himself God the Word, who is co-essential and co-eternal with the Spirit. Rather, it was the human nature that was taken up by the Word in these latter days. We would agree with him that the Spirit is the Son's own, and would accept his formula as a godly one, so long as he also says that the Spirit is of one nature with the Son and proceeds from the Father. But if he is suggesting that the Spirit derives his existence from or through the Son, such a doctrine we would reject as entirely blasphemous. For we believe the Lord when he speaks of "the Spirit which proceeds from the Father"[75] and similarly the most divine Paul when he says that "we have received not the spirit of the world, but the Spirit which is of the Father."[76]

Cyril's Defense

I explained beforehand that the meaning of the anathemas is directed specifically against Nestorius's stuttering and careless explanations. When he referred to the Holy Spirit as "this thing which bestowed such a great glory upon Christ, which caused the demons to fear him and which granted him to be taken up into heaven," and spouted such garbage as if Christ were a person just like the rest of us, the anathema became absolutely necessary, not to exclude people who say that Jesus, namely, God the Word made man, was glorified by the Holy Spirit, but in opposition to those who openly claim that he made use of a power

75. Jn 15.26.
76. 1 Cor 2.12.

that came through the Spirit and was something other than his own. After all, remember how he said quite clearly about the Holy Spirit, "He shall glorify me,"[77] and by this we know that it was because the Holy Spirit was at work within him that he could shatter evil, unclean powers; what we deny is that he made use of a power that he had through the Spirit as something that did not belong to him, just as a saint would do. No, the Spirit was and is his own, just as he in turn belongs to the Father. This is what the god-inspired Paul makes abundantly clear to us when he wrote, "Those who are in the flesh are not able to please God; but you are not in the flesh, but in the Spirit, if indeed the Spirit of God dwells in you. But if anyone does not possess the Spirit of Christ, then he does not belong to him."[78] As our Savior said, the Holy Spirit proceeds from God the Father and is not foreign to the Son, since everything is with the Father. He also taught about the Holy Spirit, "All that the Father possesses is mine; because of this I said to you that he would take from me and make it known to you."[79] The Holy Spirit, then, glorified Jesus by enacting miracles, but he did so as his own Spirit, not as some power over and above him, seeing as he is reckoned to be God.

So, then, we have not said anything offensive to angels or prophets, as this man has dared to suggest—he seems to know only how to accuse other people. Since, however, his aim (and that of his accomplices) is to divide the single Christ into two, one who is glorified and controlled, and another who does the glorifying and the controlling, they foolishly mock every godly argument that would keep them safe from such a heretical position. Moreover, this censorious individual makes a further point about the blessed Gabriel: "For he was the very first who, even before the conception, proclaimed that Christ would be born in the flesh from the Holy Spirit." This would mean, then, that there is one Christ who is in the flesh and another one who is the Word of God the Father. Where is the union in all this? What benefit could there be if we think of, or speak of, two separate individual Christs? So, if they are going to construct a

77. Jn 16.14.   78. Rom 8.8.–9.
79. Jn 16.15.

mask for themselves and talk about a single Christ while in fact they are thinking of two, then let them listen to what we have to say: "How long will you waver between two poles?"[80] It would be better to walk in a straight line and hold on to an inviolable, well-grounded faith rather than to limp along with such foolish notions as these.

♂ *Tenth Anathema*

Divine Scripture says that Christ became "the high priest and apostle of our confession"[81] and that he "offered himself for us as a sweet-smelling savor to God the Father."[82] Therefore, if any say that it was not the Word of God himself who became our high priest and apostle when he became incarnate and a man like us, but another, separate individual besides him, one born from a woman, or if any say that he brought this offering on his own behalf rather than just on our behalf (for the one who knew no sin was not in need of any offering), let them be anathema.

Theodoret's Critique

The unchangeable nature did not change into a nature of flesh. It took human nature into itself and appointed it above the level of normal high priests. This is what the blessed Paul meant when he said that "every high priest is taken from among the people and is appointed to deal with matters relating to God on the people's behalf, to offer gifts and sacrifices for sins. He is able to deal gently with those who are ignorant and going astray because he is himself subject to weakness. This is why he needs to make an offering for his own sins as well as for the people's."[83] He explains this a little further on when he says, "As

---

80. 1 Kgs 18.21. The Hebrew verse literally reads, "How long will you limp on two crutches?" metaphorically to mean "waver between two opinions/options." The LXX translates literally, but the metaphorical intention seems to have been well understood by exegetes, and Cyril uses the verse appropriately here to confront Theodoret with making a clear choice between orthodoxy and heresy.

81. Heb 3.1.   82. Eph 5.2.

83. Heb 5.1–3.

was Aaron, so was Christ."[84] So as to prove that the nature that was taken up was a weak one, he says, "During the time of his Incarnation, Jesus offered up prayers and petitions with fervent cries and tears to the one who could save him from death, and he was heard because of his godliness. Even though he was the Son, he learned obedience through what he suffered, and, after he had been made perfect, he became the source of eternal salvation for all who obey him because he was nominated by God as a high priest in the order of Melchizedek."[85]

Given all this, who is this person who was made perfect by virtuous deeds rather than being so naturally? Who is this person who learned obedience through his trials without knowing anything about it before those trials? And who is this person who lived a godly life and offered his petitions with fervent cries and tears, who was unable to save himself, but had to entreat one who was able to save him and beg to be released from death? Surely not God the Word, immortal, impassible, incorporeal, the memory of whom, as the prophet says, brings rejoicing and release from tears ("for he has wiped away every tear from every face," and another prophet elsewhere says, "I remembered God and rejoiced").[86] It is he who crowns with godliness those who dwell with him, who knows all things before they come to be. It is he who has all that belongs to the Father, who is the unchangeable image of his parent, and who shows the Father within himself. But what he took up to himself from David's seed was something mortal, passible, afraid of death. Yet even so, he was able to destroy death's power because he was united to the God who took him up to himself. It was he who walked in all righteousness and said to John, "Let it be so now; it is right for us to do this so as to fulfill all righteousness."[87] This was the one who accepted the nomination to the high priesthood in the order of Melchizedek. This was the one who was beset by his own nature's weakness; he was not the almighty Word of God. That is why the blessed Paul said a little further back, "We do not have a high priest who is unable to sympathize with our weaknesses, but one who has been tempted in every way just as we are, yet

---

84. Heb 5.4–5.
86. Is 25.8; Ps 76.4 LXX.

85. Heb 5.7–10.
87. Mt 3.15.

did not sin."[88] Hence, it was the nature that was taken from us for our sake, not the one who for our salvation had taken it; it was the one that felt our sufferings in his trial without becoming sinful. But then this is exactly the point made by the verse he refers to at the opening of this anathema: "Think about the apostle and high priest of our confession, Jesus, who was faithful to the one who created him, just as Moses also was faithful in all God's house."[89] But then no orthodox thinker would call the unmade and uncreated Word of God a creature, he who is co-eternal with the Father; whereas the man, one of us, the one who was taken up, would be so called. Neither was God the Word, who was from God himself, ordained as our high priest; it was he who was of David's seed who became our high priest and atoning sacrifice because he was sinless. He offered his very self to God for our sake because he possessed within himself God the Word, who was from God, united and connected to him inseparably.

Cyril's Defense

When Israel had offended the God of the universe and provoked him to anger, the prophet Jeremiah lamented, "Who will make my head a source of water, and my eyes a fountain of tears? Then would I weep for this people day and night."[90] Personally, I believe that these words are no more applicable to the Israelites than they are to those who cannot control their own mouths when speaking of Christ: "bold and arrogant people who are abusive of the ineffable glory," as the Scriptures have it.[91] As a result of excessive stupidity they have rejected the straight and irreproachable road of Christ-like godliness, made for themselves paths that lead in other directions, and marred the beauty of the truth with dangerous notions of their own invention. That is why they are ones who are really deserving of our mournful lamentations. These people who have opted to hold opinions so universally despicable, they should take heed when we say: "You are in error because you do not know the

88. Heb 4.15.   89. Heb 3.1–2.
90. Jer 9.1.   91. Cf. 2 Pt 2.10.

Scriptures,"[92] nor do you know the great and glorious mystery of the Incarnation. You see, the divinely inspired Scriptures declare to us that Emmanuel is God-made-man, and they assert that the Word of God the Father partook of flesh and blood like our own[93] and became flesh,[94] that is, a man, not by some sort of change or alteration, but by the power of the ineffable union. This is why we say that there is a single Lord Jesus Christ, a single faith, and a single holy baptism,[95] whereas these others have abandoned orthodoxy and set up their own proud, stubborn minds in place of the Holy Scriptures. They are interested only in what they feel like and so argue that a man was taken up by God the Word in line with what one of the holy prophets once said: "I was neither a prophet nor a prophet's son, but a herdsman, and a gatherer of sycamore fruits, and the Lord took me up from the sheep";[96] or as the blessed David said, "The Lord takes up the meek,"[97] obviously meaning a contingent spiritual possession by means of his will, grace, and sanctification, in the same way that we too are, as it says, "one spirit" because we are bound to the Lord.[98] But this is not how God was made man, nor is it how he partook of flesh and blood like our own; it is rather a case of a man being possessed by God in exactly the same way in which he does for a prophet, an apostle, or any other holy man. Was the divinely inspired Paul lying to those of us who are sanctified in the faith when he very clearly said of the Only-Begotten that, though he was rich, yet he became poor for us?[99] Surely not! For he that proclaims the truth never lies. Let us examine now the question of who this rich man was, and how he became poor. They are bold enough to believe, and to suggest, that a man was taken up by God, in which case how could such a man become poor after being decorated with honors that were above his nature, given that he was glorified? If he had not been glorified, then they would be demeaning the notion of a "taking up" by bringing it right down to the inferior level of human limitations. But the latter is an unacceptable conclu-

---

92. Mt 22.29.
93. Cf. Heb 2.14.
94. Cf. Jn 1.14.
95. Cf. Eph 4.5.
96. Am 7.14–15.
97. Ps 147.6 (146.6 LXX).
98. 1 Cor 6.17.
99. Cf. 2 Cor 8.9.

sion, so he who was taken up cannot also be he who became poor. The inescapable conclusion is that the rich man was God who entered into human poverty. How did this happen, then? Come, let us think about what it entails. We have acknowledged that he is unchangeable by nature; he did not abandon his own nature and transform into that of the flesh; he remained what he was, namely, God. Where, then, can we locate the lowliness of his poverty? Is it in the fact of one like us being taken up, as the flatterers of Nestorius's profanities have dared to suggest? What sort of poverty or self-emptying would *that* entail? All he seems to want to do is to honor a man like one of us! Since the God of the universe, in acting rightly, cannot be damaged, how could he have become poor? The answer is that, being by nature God and the Son of God the Father, he became a man and was begotten of David's seed in the flesh and so endured the limitations that are natural to a servant, namely, the humanity that is in the form of God the Father, through and in whom are all things and who is the Creator of everything. After becoming a man, those human limitations were no longer disgraceful, for once he had made becoming human acceptable, why would he then reject the means by which we could see that he had really become one of us for our sakes? Were we to detach him from human deeds and words, then there would, dare we admit, be no difference between us and those who completely deprive him of his flesh, who do not believe in the divinely inspired Scripture, and who completely throw out the mystery of the Incarnation, the salvation and hope of the world, the faith, and the Resurrection.

It is equally possible, of course, that someone will object that it is belittling and inappropriate that God the Word should cry out, or be afraid of death, that he should pray against taking the cup of suffering or be appointed to the office of priesthood. Yes, I would agree. Such things are somewhat ignoble by comparison with the transcendent divine nature and glory, but it is precisely in them that we can see the poverty that he willingly endured for us. Whenever you find the dishonor arising from his self-emptying to be a problem, wonder all the more greatly at how much the Son loves us; you say that it is something mean, but he willingly did it for your sake. He wept like a man to protect your own tears. For salvation's sake he was afraid and at times allowed his flesh to suffer as it ought to, so that he might render us less fearful; he prayed that the cup be taken away, so that the cross might condemn the Jews' godlessness; in his humanity he was called weak, so that he might put a stop to your weakness; in prayer he reached up even in supplication, so that he might declare the Father's ear to be accessible even to your prayers. He slept, so that you might learn not to sleep when tempted, but rather to reach out in prayer. He even reproached the sleeping holy apostles and said, "Did you not have the strength to keep watch with me for one hour? Watch and pray so that you will not fall into temptation."[100] He set forth his own actions as an example of holy living for the benefit of everyone on earth. Why did he thus make human weakness his very own? It was so that we might believe that he really did become a man while still remaining what he was, God. What I cannot understand is how these men feign to acknowledge a single Christ, Son, and Lord, that the same individual is both God and man, while refusing to call the Word begotten of God, after he had become a man, the high priest and apostle of our confession. Instead of this they go on to assert that he should simply be called an individual man from David's seed. Presumably they are afraid that they might actually make light of Nestorius's heresy and get caught thinking along the right lines! This is what Nestorius said:

This man is the one who was made a faithful high priest toward God (for he came into existence, not pre-existing eternally); this was the man—you heretic!—who progressed little by little towards the dignity of high priesthood.

Then, so as to confirm the truth of this (or so he thought), he concluded by saying:

It was about this that John proclaimed in the Gospels, "Jesus advanced in maturity, wisdom, and grace."[101]

100. Mt 26.40.
101. Lk 2.52.

And then also:

Do not turn away from faith in the only one who is our compassionate high priest, our kinsman, our foundation. For he was sent as the blessing that was promised to Abraham's seed, so as to offer the sacrifice of his body on his own behalf, and on behalf of his race.

The most ardent fan of this nonsense of Nestorius's is of course our good friend Theodoret, who is not embarrassed to write that:

[The divine nature] took human nature into itself and appointed it above the level of normal high priests, as Paul said, "Every high priest is taken from among the people and is appointed to deal with matters relating to God on the people's behalf. He is able to deal gently with those who are ignorant and going astray because he is himself subject to weakness. This is why he needs to make an offering for his own sins as well as for the people's." [Heb 5.1–3]

Has he not gone here as far as he wanted and made out that Emmanuel is a man just like us? Are not his ideas and those others we have just mentioned closely related, and do they not give birth to just as awful a blasphemy? Tell me now, are you not afraid of what manner of priesthood belonged to Christ our universal Savior? Would you say that, because of the plan of salvation, it is inappropriate that God the Word should carry out a priest's function in a human way? Throw off the mask and deny, without pretense, that the Word became man and that this is why he may also be called high priest. Do you see him sacrificing to the Father, as if to some other, better God? Have you watched him sacrificing the whole burnt offerings in the same way as do those who have been selected from among men, who are able to deal gently with those who are ignorant and going astray because they themselves are subject to human weakness? Have you not realized that he consecrates everybody's faith, meaning their confession of faith in himself and in the all-holy Father? Tell me, is it not part of a human priest's function to require faith of those who have offered themselves in the Spirit as a sweet-smelling savor?[102] See how there is another way that he is God, even if one allows that he carries out a human priest's

102. Cf. Eph 5.2.

activity for the sake of the plan of salvation, for he sits together
with God the Father and may be visualized in his magnificence
upon the heavenly throne. Does the fact of his humanity cause
you confusion? Does the fact that he is also divine not release
you from those fears? You do not allow yourself to see how these
things show that Emmanuel is both God and man, but instead
carry on blindly rampaging far beyond the very worst godlessness in saying that he was perfected in his virtue through his
actions, and that he progressed little by little towards the dignity of high priesthood. If he so progressed, how can he have
emptied himself or become poor? If he is perfected in virtue,
then obviously he must have become perfect from a previous
state of imperfection and over a period of time; but whatever is
in a state of imperfection of virtue must lie under conviction of
guilt, and what is guilty lies under sin. In which case, how can it
be written about him that he did not commit sin?[103] You dared
to write the following:

Who is this person (he means the one who is the priest) who was made
perfect by virtuous deeds rather than being so naturally? Who is this
person who learned obedience through his trials without knowing anything about it before those trials? And who is this person who lived a
godly life and offered his petitions with fervent cries and tears, who
was unable to save himself, but had to entreat one who was able to save
him?

What a brazen and outrageous thing to say! How many tears
need we to shed to cleanse of sin all who choose to think that
way? If you accept the union, how can you not know that your
discussion was really about God made man? He humbled himself for your sake, yet you profanely proclaim, "Be it far from
you; Lord, may this never be to you," upon hearing which he
retorts, "Get behind me, Satan; you are a stumbling block to
me."[104] But then at the end of his argument he says:

[I]t was he who was of David's seed who was our high priest ... because
he possessed within himself God the Word ... united and connected to
him inseparably.

103. Cf. 1 Pt 2.22.
104. Mt 16.22–23.

How can you say that God the Word was united to the one from David's seed, if you have already attributed the priesthood to the latter only? If the union is a genuine one, then there can in no way be two; Christ is to be understood only as a single, solitary individual arising out of both.

It is therefore quite clear that they are only pretending to believe in the union. They creep up on the unwary, when they are really thinking in terms of an external, contingent connection, something that can be said of us as well since we are proclaimed by the Spirit to be in fellowship with his divine nature. So pay absolutely no attention to all this stuff and nonsense of theirs, but instead focus on the orthodox, blameless faith, and the words of the evangelists and apostles.

ཊ *Eleventh Anathema*

If any do not confess that the Lord's flesh has the power to give life and that it belongs to the Word of God the Father himself, but think that it belongs to another individual besides him who is connected to him as a matter of honor, or as if he were merely in possession of a divine indwelling, rather than, as we already said, that it is life-giving because it has become a property of the Word, who has the strength to give life to all, let them be anathema.

Theodoret's Critique

In my opinion he is deliberately making the whole thing too complicated so as to cover up his heterodoxy and so that no one will notice that his doctrine is the same as that of the heretics. But there is nothing stronger than the truth, which blows away the clouds of deceit with its own beams of light. Thus enlightened, we shall now prove his doctrine to be unorthodox. First of all, he never refers to the flesh as being "rational," nor does he ever acknowledge that the man who was taken up was a whole man. Instead, he always merely says "flesh," just as is the case in the Apollinarian doctrines. Furthermore, interspersed among his arguments he introduces the idea of "mixture,"

Theodoret's Critique

The property of suffering belongs to that which is passible. The impassible is above suffering. Therefore, it was the form of the servant that suffered, the form of God of course being together with it. The latter allowed the former to experience suffering because salvation is born of suffering, and he made those sufferings his very own by being united to them. So it was not God who suffered. It was the man, one of us, whom God had taken up. This is also why the blessed Isaiah predicted that he would "be a man of affliction and well acquainted with pain."[110] Even Christ the Master himself asked the Jews, "Why do you seek to kill me, a *man* who has told you the truth?"[111] It is not the one who has life in himself who is killed. It is the one who possesses the mortal nature. This is what the Lord taught on another occasion when he said, "Destroy this temple, and in three days I shall raise it up."[112] So the one who was of David was destroyed, while the Only-Begotten, God the Word, he who was born impassibly of the Father before the ages, raised up the one that was destroyed.

Cyril's Defense

Of course I agree that the nature of the Word is impassible. I would think that everyone is well aware of this, nor would be so crazy as to suggest that the ineffable nature (which is really above all natures), which is in no way capable of suffering, was possessed by human weaknesses. The whole plan of redemption must have been ingeniously designed since suffering brought about the salvation of the world, even though it is impossible for the Word who is begotten of God to suffer in respect of his own nature. For he made the passible body his very own, the result of which is that one can say that he suffered by means of something naturally passible, even while he himself remains impassible in respect of his own nature; and since he willingly suffered in the flesh, for this very reason he is called, and actually is, the Savior of all. It is just as Paul says, "By the grace of God he tasted death

110. Is 53.3.   111. Jn 8.40.
112. Jn 2.19.

on behalf of all."[113] The divinely inspired Peter will testify to the same thing, rightly saying, "since Christ suffered for us,"[114] not in his divine nature, but in his flesh. In what way, then, can we say that the Lord of glory has been crucified?[115] How is it that the one through whom and in whom everything exists (as the blessed Paul has it)[116] is appointed by God the Father as the head of the body, the church, and how is it that he became also the first-born from the dead?[117] Surely it was because he took personal ownership of the sufferings that pertained to his own flesh. The Lord of glory could not have become a normal person like us. Maybe, however, you would at least say this, that the fact of the union is enough to demonstrate that the single Christ is to be identified with the crucified Lord. Therefore, let them predicate all these things of him and confess that God the Word is the Savior who remains impassible in his divine nature while also suffering in the flesh, just as Peter said. For the body that tasted death belonged to him because the union was totally genuine. How else would he be "a Jew in respect of the flesh, Christ who is God over all and forever blessed, amen"?[118] Into whose death were we baptized? Whose resurrection do we acknowledge when we are justified? Although in respect of his own nature God the Word is above dying, he is actually life itself. Were we, then, baptized into the death of an ordinary man? And is it in *him* that we put our trust and are justified? Or do we, in fact, proclaim the death of God made man, who suffered death in his flesh for us? Do we escape the grief caused by sin through his resurrection? For we were bought "at a price," "not with corruptible things, silver or gold, but with the precious blood of Christ, as of a lamb without guilt or stain."[119] It would not be hard to say lots more than this on the subject, and we could provide citations from the holy Fathers, but these things, I deem, will suffice for those who are keen to understand. After all, it is written, "Grant a wise man an opportunity, and he will become wiser; instruct a just man, and he will accept further instruction."[120]

---

113. Heb 2.9.

114. 1 Pt 4.1.

115. Cf. 1 Cor 2.8.

116. Cf. Heb 2.10.

117. Cf. Col 1.17–18.

118. Rom 9.5.

119. 1 Cor 6.20; 1 Pt 1.18–19.

120. Prv 9.9.

A DEFENSE OF THE TWELVE
ANATHEMAS AGAINST THE BISHOPS
OF THE DIOCESE OF ORIENS

Prologue

EOPLE WHO focus their thoughts upon the most holy God and who choose to speak on the side of true doctrine reject the impure and empty words of the unholy heretics while their inner eye, hidden as it is deep within their hearts, remains fixed upon the divinely inspired Scriptures. They thereby fill their hearts with wholesome ideas and set their faces against those who distort the truth, and very vigorously too, as if they were saying, "We have been very zealous for the Lord."[1] Now, since Nestorius has been splurting out all his ill-considered speeches against Christ, the Savior of us all, and has been stirring up from its very foundations that supreme issue itself, the mystery of the Incarnation, we got to the point where we would have to fight for the doctrines of the faith, especially as it would be extremely risky to remain silent on such a matter and also because we were getting absolutely nowhere by our frequent warnings to him to desist from such blasphemies. We therefore picked out his main arguments and then resolutely anathematized them, or rather, all those who would subscribe to them, being as we were persuaded by the blessed Paul, who said, "If anyone preaches to you contrary to what you received, let him be anathema; and even if we or an angel from heaven should preach to you contrary to what you received, let him be anathema."[2] Now, I do not know whether the people who seem to be so critical of this action of ours are so because they

1. 1 Kgs 19.14.
2. Gal 1.9, 8.

share Nestorius's opinions or because, although officially they reject his doctrine, they are nonetheless trying as far as possible to ally themselves with him and to make out that it is we, who are trying to mount a defense of Christ our Savior, who are the ones who should be vilified! One can only assume that his attacks on false teaching recommended themselves to them as evidence of a genuine love for Christ. Even now they have not acted as they should. How so? By making enemies out of those very people who, had they imitated them instead, would have received the crown of incorruptibility as well. And so they launched their attack on my anathemas as being ill-conceived and wrote something against each of them in turn—the conclusions and incomprehensible ramblings of their own minds. They thought to beguile their readers and anyone else that might chance unprepared upon their writings. That is why we felt obliged to place truth in the frontline and repel their attack, thereby to unmask our opponents as mere conflict-mongers and prove that truth-seekers are their enemies. So, in what follows, each section is headed by one of the anathemas, to which we have appended their comments followed by our own thoughts. In doing so we are making use of the divine Scriptures as our skilled judges, and we request a fair and blameless judgment from those who know the truth.

೪♥ First Anathema

If any do not confess Emmanuel to be truly God and, on this basis, the holy Virgin to be the "Mother-of-God" (since she bore in the flesh the Word of God made flesh), let them be anathema.

The Orientals' Critique

Who would really agree with him that the Word of God made flesh was born "in the flesh"? For if she gave birth "in the flesh," it would no longer have been as a virgin. And if (as he maintains) she gave birth as a virgin rather than in a way that is proper to the divine, what would we then do with the verse that says, "The Holy Spirit will come over you and the power of the

Most High will overshadow you"?[3] How could it have been that the star miraculously appeared and pointed her out? Or how could the Magi have traversed Persia under its guidance, sought out the child, found it, and then offered their gifts both to him whom they recognized as well as to him whom they physically saw? Or how could angels have descended from heaven onto the nativity, have intermingled with shepherds, and have sung, "Glory to God in the highest, and upon earth peace, goodwill among men"?[4] Do such facts relate to a birth "in the flesh" or to one that is proper to the divine? On the other hand, were we heedlessly to fall in with what he is saying, then we would have to imagine a change in the Word, a transformation into flesh, and thereby to suppose that he became both "a sin and a curse,"[5] if, that is, we fail to attend to what follows logically from his propositions and to what they presuppose, as well as the usage of Scripture itself. We understand instead that, in line with the Gospels' meaning, the Word's "becoming" flesh is really a "tabernacling" in the flesh.

Cyril's Defense

Wise John clarifies the mystery of salvation brought about by the Incarnation of the Only-Begotten when he writes, "and the Word became flesh and tabernacled among us."[6] The blessed Fathers who met that time at Nicaea understood this correctly and so said that he, the Word born of God the Father, the one through whom the Father made all things, Light from Light, true God from true God, became flesh and became a man, that is, that he was united to flesh that possessed rational soul and that he became a man while also remaining God. There is no one who doubts that the union came about without change or confusion, while, as I said, the Word of God remained what he is, even though he became flesh (since he is unalterable by nature). For what is said to have "become flesh" did not change into the nature of flesh, but is rather thought of as existing alongside the flesh and being united to it.

3. Lk 1.35.   4. Lk 2.14.
5. 2 Cor 5.21; Gal 3.3.   6. Jn 1.14.

This is what the blessed Fathers were thinking of when they gave the holy Virgin the title of "Mother-of-God." They believed that she bore the Son, become flesh and become a man, the very one through whom the Father made all things. Nestorius, who came up with these blasphemies that were quite new to us, opposed this understanding and decided that the title "Mother-of-God" was totally inappropriate. I quote:

I often asked them, "Are you suggesting that the blessed Virgin gave birth to the divinity?" Immediately they recoil from the expression, and respond, "No, who would be so disgustingly blasphemous as to say that the woman who gave birth to the temple also created God within herself by the Spirit?" If I then go on to ask, "What, then, is wrong with my suggesting that we abandon this title and agree on the normal way of indicating the two natures?" then this way of putting things is suddenly considered to be blasphemous! Either be transparent and confess that blessed Mary gave birth to the divinity, or else, if you are prepared to abandon this title as blasphemous, why then do you pretend that you have not said the very things that I have myself said?

He is playing a game! He is profanely seducing those who call the Virgin "Mother-of-God" into thinking that they must thereby necessarily confess that the pure and self-subsistent divine nature became a fruit of the flesh and that it was the woman who gave rise to the Word of God's very existence! We want to make it quite clear that we wholly reject any such position. We are not so foolish as willfully to think what one ought not to. What we do say, however, is that according to the Scriptures the Virgin gave birth to the Word of God, which had become flesh, that is, a man, and further that she bore him "in the flesh," that is, "in the manner of the flesh." It was God the Father who divinely begot the Son, who was also God, from his own self. Since "what is begotten of flesh is flesh,"[7] the Virgin, being as she was flesh, begot in the flesh. By calling it "in the flesh" one is not denying the miracle of his nativity, nor is one making redundant that power of the Holy Spirit by which he formed the infant within his mother. Rather, it is simply to teach that, just as God, in line with his own nature, begets divinely, that is, in a manner proper to the divine, so also a man begets in a manly way, or flesh in a

7. Jn 3.6.

fleshly way. Seeing as the Word is by nature God, even when he became flesh, he must have come forth in a manner that is proper to the divine, that is, as befits one who is truly God. After all, he is the only person whose mother had never had intercourse; and she, who gave birth to him in the flesh, remained a virgin.

So I am astonished that the very people who shrink from calling the holy Virgin "Mother-of-God" still say that she gave birth in a manner proper to the divine.[8] After all, a normal man is not born in such a way. They also mention that the Magi "offered their gifts both to him whom they recognized as well as to him whom they physically saw." But in saying so, they are dividing the one Lord Jesus Christ into a duality after the union. He whom they recognized became visible not because his nature had been transformed, but because he was united to the visible body.

If so, then how can the sacred Scripture say that the holy apostles "became eye-witnesses and servants of the Word,"[9] when it is manifestly obvious that the Word of God the Father is incorporeal and intangible? I may note also that the holy disciples said, "that which was from the beginning, which we have heard, which we have seen, which we have looked at with our eyes, and which our hands have touched, concerning the Word of life."[10] Therefore, these gifts must have been offered to a single individual, that is, to Christ, insofar as the same individual is at the same time both God and man. This is why there were choirs of holy angels at his nativity, and armies of spirits proclaiming him Savior and Redeemer.

Now when in considering the evangelist's expression, "the Word became flesh,"[11] they claim to be worried that, by keeping to the precise meaning of the term "became," they are implying that some sort of change occurred within the divine nature, I do applaud their concern, but am shocked that they therefore distance themselves from the expression and from its correct

8. In Andrew's critique, being born "in a manner proper to the divine" was set up as mutually exclusive to being born "in the flesh." Cyril, of course, asserts that both are true in the case of the Incarnation.

9. Lk 1.2.   10. 1 Jn 1.1.

11. Jn 1.14.

and required meaning, and that they make out that to say "the Word became flesh" amounts to saying that he became "a curse and a sin"![12] How can they not have realized that the blessed evangelist, while using the expression "became," excluded any notion of change by immediately adding the words, "and he tabernacled among us"? Even to dare the suggestion that the Word became flesh in such a way that he could actually be said to have become a sin and a curse is both absurd and illogical.

In reality he did not himself "become" either a sin or a curse. He was, however, "counted among the lawless,"[13] despite being innocent, so as to abolish sin,[14] and he was called "accursed,"[15] despite being the one who blessed creation, so as to remove the curse that hangs over us and set free from punishment those who believe in him. So, strictly speaking, he did not become a curse and a sin, but rather he was given these names so that he might abolish both the curse and the sin. Had he after all become flesh in that sort of way, he would thereby have abolished the flesh as well as the sin and the curse. He would not have become a man or been truly incarnate. The mystery would have been a matter of appearance only; his becoming a man would have been purely nominal, and any hope of resurrection would have been obliterated once and for all. Into whose death were we baptized?[16] Where is the "word of faith which we proclaimed"?[17] For we are saved by confessing that Jesus is Lord and believing that "God raised him from the dead."[18] Have we placed our faith in a mere man, someone just like one of us? Are we no longer to worship the Word who appeared among us in human form?[19] Did he not take upon himself the servant's form even though, as God, he was free? Did he not humble himself, despite having a right to divine transcendence? He shares his form with the Father, he is on the level of the Father, and did he not condescend to empty himself, all the while bestowing his beneficence upon creation out of his very own resources?

---

12. 2 Cor 5.21 and Gal 3.13, as quoted by Andrew in his critique.

13. Lk 22.37; Is 53.12.   14. Cf. Rom 6.6.

15. Gal 3.13.   16. Cf. Rom 6.3.

17. Rom 10.8.   18. Rom 10.9.

19. Phil 2.7.

Let us be rid of such stupid ideas. The blessed Fathers initiated us into the mysteries in a quite different way. They said that the Word of God the Father was made flesh and genuinely became a man, without change or confusion, although just how this mystery occurred cannot really be put into words. As a testimony of what I have said, I shall quote some of the things that these Fathers have written:

The testimony of Peter, bishop of Alexandria:

So the evangelist quite rightly says that "the Word became flesh and tabernacled among us."[20] It is clear that this is why the angel could greet the Virgin by saying, "Greetings, favored one, the Lord is with you."[21] Now what Gabriel said was, "the Lord is with you," not, "God the Word is with you." The implication is that he was begotten within his mother and that he became flesh, as it is written, "The Holy Spirit shall come over you and the power of the Most High will overshadow you; for this reason he who is born is holy and shall be called God's Son."[22]

The testimony of Athanasius, archbishop of Alexandria:

So, since the flesh was begotten of Mary, Mother-of-God, he himself, who brings other things into existence, is said to have been born so that he might make our birth[23] his own.[24]

The testimony of Athanasius again, from his letter to Epictetus:

How did so-called Christians even consider doubting whether the Lord, who came out of Mary, while being essentially and naturally God's Son, is also, in his flesh, from David's seed and from holy Mary's flesh, while some have been so rash as to suggest that Christ, who suffered and was crucified in the flesh, is neither Lord, nor Savior, nor God, nor is he the Father's Son? Or how can people who say that the Word has descended onto a holy man, as if he were just a prophet instead of actually becoming a man by taking a body from Mary, hope to call themselves Christians? They are suggesting that Christ is one individual while the Word of God, who before Mary and for all eternity was the Father's Son, is a different individual! How can people who say that the Son is one thing and the Word of God something else really be Christians?[25]

It is these judgments of the holy Fathers that have been our lead. Anyone who teaches otherwise or harbors a different opin-

---

20. Jn 1.14.
22. Lk 1.35.
24. Athanasius, *Contra Arianos* 3.33.

21. Lk 1.28.
23. Or possibly, "our origin."
25. Athanasius, *Ad Epictetum* 2.

ion is veering off the main highway. The following quotation demonstrates that it was quite normal for the holy Fathers to say that Christ was begotten "in the flesh"; hence it is all the more appropriate for everyone else, not least ourselves. It goes like this:

Of the bishop of Iconium:

You could never be begotten in the Spirit unless he had been begotten in the flesh. If he did not adopt the form of the servant, you could never attain to the glory of being adopted as children.[26]

Hence it is quite clear that the expression "in the flesh" is simply equivalent to "according to the flesh" in just the same way that the expression "in the divinity" is equivalent to "according to the divinity."[27]

❧ Third Anathema

If any divide the concrete existences of the one Christ after the union, connecting them with a connection that is merely one of dignity, authority, or power, rather than by a convergence at the level of a natural union, let them be anathema.

The Orientals' Critique

Let us recall once more something that he himself[28] said in his first treatise which implied that he was speaking of two concrete existences:

In terms of his very own nature, the Word from God the Father has not been sanctified on his own. If there is anyone who thinks that the one born of the holy Virgin was anointed and sanctified on his own, then this is why he was given the name of "Christ."[29]

---

26. Amphilochius of Iconium, *Frag.* 3, from a work entitled *On the Nativity according to Flesh*, ed. C. Datema, *Amphilochii Iconiensis opera* (Turnhout: Brepols, 1978).

27. Cyril is showing that the Greek expressions *sarkikôs* and *kata sarka* are synonyms.

28. I.e., Cyril.

29. *Ep.* 1 (*To the Monks*) 15–16. The excerpt quoted here is grammatically incomplete. Cyril fills out the citation below. See p. 141.

So how is it, then, that he has now forgotten what he said and is combining the natures into a single concrete existence, confusing them and calling the divine union "natural"? Who would ever accept the idea that the divine union, which was part of the mystery of God's salvation plan, is "natural"? If the union were a "natural" one, where does that leave grace? Where does it leave the divine mystery? We have been teaching that, because the natures have been appointed by the God who appoints all things, they must of necessity be subservient to logical consequences. Or will the whole plan of salvation turn out, by some sort of revolution of natural logic, to be in line with that notorious man Apollinarius's ridiculous and fabulous views about the millennium?[30]

Cyril's Defense

Paul, who is God's mouthpiece, in his role as steward of the divine mysteries and the one through whom Christ himself speaks,[31] clarified for everyone just how the Only-Begotten Word of God became a man. He says, "For surely it was not angels he took for himself, but Abraham's seed; that is why he had to become like his brothers in every way, so that he might become a merciful and faithful high priest with respect to God."[32] Our statements are protected by absolutely orthodox judgments. We are constantly guided by the divinely inspired Scriptures, and we hold what the Fathers have said in the highest esteem.[33] In fact we treat that as divine law. We therefore deny that the Word of God the Father took for himself either the nature of the holy angels or even his own nature. Instead, in line with what the Holy Scriptures say, we believe that he overshadowed the holy Virgin (that is, the power of the Most High Father did)[34] and

---

30. Apollinarius was charged by Basil (*Ep.* 263.4) with a literalist view of the millennium in which "we will become Jews once again." Andrew is suggesting that, because Cyril's view of the union has robbed Christian salvation of its effectiveness, it has a similar effect to Apollinarius's eschatology.

31. 1 Cor 4.1; 2 Cor 3.13.

32. Heb 2.16–17.

33. "Fathers": *theêgorôn*, lit., "those who speak for God," which sometimes refers to the authors of Scripture, sometimes to the Fathers of the Church.

34. Lk 1.35.

formed for himself a body from her, albeit through the working of the Holy Spirit, and became a man and was called son of Abraham and of David. He did not in any way, by becoming a man, cease to be what he truly is, the Son of God the Father; rather, even when he became flesh, he remained in his divine nature, transcendence, and glory, because, as God, he is unalterable and above all change. He is, then, one and the same subject, Son and Lord, both before and after the Incarnation. To divide the single Son into two, and thereby to dissolve the genuineness of the union by splitting it up into bits, putting the man over here and the god over there, separate from each other, is an offense of the very highest sacrilege. Nestorius had something like this in mind when he dared to say the following:

"May you have the same attitude as did Christ Jesus, who, although he was in God's form, did not intend to grasp at equality with God; instead he emptied himself by taking the form of a servant."[35] Paul does not here say, "May you have the same attitude as did God the Word who, although being in God's form, took upon himself a servant's form"; instead, he takes "Christ" as a name that connotes both of the natures. He avoids any risk by saying that he took upon himself the servant's form and calling him God, dividing up the expressions between the two in a way that cannot be faulted.[36]

In another explanation, he says,

"That at the name of Jesus every knee will bow, those in heaven and those on earth and those under the ground, and every tongue will confess that Jesus Christ is Lord."[37] I revere him who is borne for the sake of the bearer; I worship the visible for the sake of the hidden. God is indivisible from him who is visible. I do not divide the honor of him who is indivisible. I divide the natures, but I unite the worship.[38]

And then in a further explanation,

35. Phil 2.5–7.
36. A quotation from Nestorius's first sermon against the title "Mother-of-God"; see F. Loofs, ed., *Nestoriana, Die Fragmente des Nestorius* (Halle, 1905), 254,5–12.
37. Phil 2.10–11.
38. Another quotation from the same sermon (Loofs, *Nestoriana*, 261,20–262,6). This was a well-quoted passage, used, for example, both in Cyril's *Third Letter to Nestorius* (*Ep.* 17) and in his *Letter to Acacius of Melitene* (*Ep.* 40) to indict the bishop of Constantinople.

Call him who assumes, God; add that the one who is assumed is the form of a servant; then introduce the honor due to their being connected, that they both hold their authority in common, that the honor is the same for both. Acknowledge the unity of the honor, even though the natures both persist.

Do you see how he is always splitting up the natures, even while he says that he "unites the worship," refers to their authority as being "in common," and calls their unity merely one "of honor"? But if something is held in common, it cannot be common to one, but always to two or more things understood to be individual and separate. So why, then, have they thrown such an enormous accusation against a statement that so effectively anathematizes all such things? What is so absurd about our rightful concern to protect our brothers and sisters by opposing sound doctrine to those disgusting and inopportune statements of Nestorius?[39]

Now, since they claim that I contradict myself, and to prove this they have quoted from my letter to the holy monks, I think I ought to make some pointed remarks in response. They say that even "he himself" talks about two concrete existences, and they seem to reckon the fact that we have opted to use the same words as they would to be quite some rebuke. First I must quote in full the relevant part of the letter, and then I shall add some more so as to show just how they have deliberately misrepresented everything. I quote:

In terms of his very own nature, the Word of God the Father has not been sanctified on his own. If there is anyone who thinks that the one born of the holy Virgin was anointed and sanctified on his own, and that this explains why he was given the name "Christ," then let him go on and explain how this anointing would suffice to prove that the one being anointed shared equally in the honor due to God who is over all, and that he sits on the same throne.[40]

This Nestorius, who keeps making up ever new profanities, frequently asserted that the Word of God is individually named "Christ," while he to whom the holy Virgin gave birth is another

39. Loofs, *Nestoriana*, 354,7–11.

40. *Ep.* 1 (*To the Monks*) 15–16. Cyril now quotes the whole sentence, which was grammatically incomplete in the previously quoted version. See n. 29, p. 138.

Christ, a separate individual. That is why we dismissed any such doctrine outright as totally degrading as well as being miles off the truth, and we have asserted instead that the Word of God the Father, considered on his own, was neither anointed with the oil of joy by himself, nor was there some other son who existed wholly on his own as a man, alongside the Word of God, and who came from the holy Virgin. In fact, we insist that everyone confess Christ to be one, the Only-Begotten Word of God made flesh and made man, for "there is one Lord, one faith, one baptism."[41] So it is absolutely obvious to anyone who normally holds orthodox opinions that these people have falsified my intentions in writing the above, and that they are thereby slandering the truth.

Furthermore, looked at from a different point of view, there would be nothing contradictory in thinking that, at the level of nature, the flesh is something quite different from the Word that was begotten of God the Father. In fact it would be perfectly reasonable to think so, and could not be gainsaid. And of course the Only-Begotten is, in turn, something different at the level of his own nature. But to acknowledge this is not the same as separating the natures after they have been united. Anyone who really wanted to come to grips with the real meaning of this mystery and get to the bottom of it would appreciate what I said at the start, that what the Word (being God) took to himself was not his own nature but Abraham's seed;[42] and also that his holy body, which is of Abraham's seed and which the man took from the holy Virgin when he emerged, the purpose of which was that the Only-Begotten might become like his brothers and be called the firstborn,[43] is not consubstantial with the Word that was begotten of God. Even though, however, the body and the Word of God the Father belong to different natures, there is still only a single Christ and Son, God and Lord, despite his becoming flesh. This idea of dissolving the means by which a genuine union occurred by keeping the concrete existences apart is very damaging. They end up each as a separate individual, connected by nothing but an external relationship based on degrees of honor.

41. Eph 4.5.   42. Cf. Heb 2.16.
43. Cf. Heb 2.17; Rom 8.29.

If we were to refer to the union as "natural," we would be speaking accurately since the divinely inspired Scriptures usually use the term in just this way. Paul, for example, God's mouthpiece, wrote somewhere, "We were children of wrath by nature, as also are the rest."[44] Now no one would ever say that God's anger is really something that is "by nature," and so imply that sinners should be thought of literally as its children, else we would turn out to be no different from those who are diseased with Manichaeism. Rather, the expression "by nature" here simply means "in truth."

So then, we affirm that the union occurred "naturally" out of two unequal elements, divinity and humanity, without thereby either confusing or blending the natures together, despite what our opponents might say. We also consistently insist that there is a single Christ, Son, and Lord. We have nothing to do with Apollinarian doctrine, for we must keep our distance from those who have already been condemned for bringing the truth into disrepute.

?❧ Fourth Anathema

If any allocate the sayings in the evangelical and apostolic writings to two persons, or concrete existences, whether those spoken by the saints about Christ or those he used about himself, and then attribute some of them to a man who is thought of separately from the Word of God, and others only to the Word of God because they are more appropriate to God, let them be anathema.

The Orientals' Critique

It is important now to recall some of his very own pronouncements. He wrote:

Even when you hear that "he advanced in age and wisdom and grace,"[45] you should not think that it follows that God's Word progressed towards being wise, nor should you be so rash as to suggest,

44. Eph 2.3.
45. Lk 2.52.

without thinking, that this increase in age, wisdom, and grace is simply attributable to the man.[46]

Even though Cyril is here denying the very witness of Scripture, which actually teaches that this growth occurred in terms of the Lord's visible flesh, we do not need here and now to make a full refutation of this anathema, since what we have already said above shows that he speaks in terms of two concrete existences, and that he contradicts himself.

But there is absolutely no need at all to match up different verses to two different persons, or to two concrete existences, or two sons, which would mean dividing up the union, the single Son. Whatever sort of argument or methodology you use, the perfect union simply cannot be divided, nor can the single Son. Now because we have held onto this perfect union by agreeing to the formula of one Son and Christ and Lord, everything that is said about him must be taken as being said about this one, individual Son. So it is the significance of the united natures that makes it appropriate to predicate all these expressions of the Son. But does he really need to be so extreme in his refusal to divide up the various things that are said in the Gospels, whether it be those that the Lord says about himself or those that are quoted in the apostles' writings?

You see, if we do not categorize these expressions at all, then how would we oppose the Eunomians and Arians who blend all the sayings together, put them under a single nature, and so blasphemously introduce human baseness into the transcendent nature of unsullied divinity? And what are we supposed to think about all those things that the Lord said because he had a visible, fleshly nature, such as, "I did not come to do my own will," and, "I received the command as to what to say and what to speak," and, "I do nothing of myself," and, "I am going to my Father and your Father, to my God and your God," and so forth?[47] Although the sayings remain indivisible just as the natures are, God is the Father of the Only-Begotten God

46. Cyril, *Paschal Letter* 17.3.65–71; see *Cyrille d'Alexandrie, Lettres Festales*, ed. W. H. Burns et al., Sources chrétiennes 372 (Paris: Éditions du Cerf, 1991), 278. Also FOTC 127, p. 67.

47. Jn 6.38; 12.49; 8.28; 20.17.

on his own account, and it is on the basis of his divinity that the Son serves and ministers to his Father's commands. If we were to understand that the human baseness belonged to the divine nature, then to whom would we attribute such expressions as, "I and the Father are one," or places where he says that he acts in line with the Father, such as, "for just as the Father raises the dead, so also the Son makes alive everyone he wants to," meaning, of course, not just those he is told to?[48]

Now of course it is quite true that, just as the Lord himself said, the Father is both God and Father. He is God of the flesh who, in the latter days, came from David's seed; and he is the Father of the Word of God, who was impassibly and eternally begotten of him, even while we take great care to acknowledge that this sonship exists in a single figure. What is more, if we do not divide up these expressions at all, how would we understand the pronouncements, "Truly, truly I say to you, before Abraham existed, I am," and, "Everything came into being through him"?[49] Do we attribute these facts, namely, that he existed prior to Abraham and David and that all things came to exist through him, to the nature that came into being from David's seed in the latter days? Should we not rather quite properly insist that, even while we do not mix up the natures nor in any way divide up the union, the expressions should be matched up according to the significance of the two natures that have been united, just as we said before? They should be attributed to a single Son, Lord, and Christ, of course, but we do not just compress everything into a single nature!

What about verses such as, "No one has ascended into heaven except the one who comes down from heaven, the Son of Man, who is in heaven," and, "What, then, if you see the Son of Man ascend where he was not previously"?[50] In these cases we may recognize each nature under a single name because of that perfect union that no one can truly understand. The expression "Son of Man" must surely mean that which has been united to him in a way that neither confuses the two nor splits them up. Now, if he was calling himself "Son of Man" because he had

48. Jn 10.30; 5.19; 5.21.   49. Jn 8.58; 1.3.
50. Jn 3.13; 6.62.

taken upon himself a visible, fleshly nature, then it is just as true that he proved by his deeds that he is God. So we have, "Jesus Christ, through whom are all things," and, "Jesus Christ, yesterday and today the same, and forever."[51] If he is "yesterday and today," how can "all things be through him"? And if "all things are through him," how can he be "yesterday and today"? The expressions, "all things are through him," "yesterday and today," and "the same forever," can all be trustworthy and genuine only so long as we match these expressions up in accordance with the different natures, which have themselves been united in a way that neither confuses the two nor splits them up. We realize that "yesterday and today" has to do with the visible nature, while "forever" has to do with the hidden nature. Because of the individuality of his Sonship, they are one and the same.

Cyril's Defense

These people who simply want to censure the anathemas, which are so crucial as far as we are concerned, without properly examining them, are not interested in talking about the truth. Their only purpose seems to be to make a real display of their excessively critical mentality. Were they to fasten their rather feeble and pedantic thoughts upon the Scriptures, they would realize that, far from proving that I wrote this anathema without any real understanding, they are in fact reinforcing it by their formulae and their arguments. How so, I ask? Well, that excellent friend of ours, Nestorius, when he was preaching in church, said something like this:

To say it as clearly as I can for everyone: the followers of Arius, Eunomius, and Apollinarius, as well as all of those who belong to their family, are very keen to use the title Mother-of-God because, by allowing for mixture and undivided natures, then none of the baseness associated with humanity need be implicated in divinity. They are able to preserve his sphere against any involvement with divinity by making out that everything said of him is said of a single subject.[52]

51. 1 Cor 8.6; Heb 13.8.
52. Loofs, *Nestoriana*, 273,5–12. This citation is taken from an oft-quoted sermon of Nestorius's. A longer version of the same passage is quoted at the

When we have Nestorius saying things like this, the anathema becomes all the more vital for preventing the one Lord Jesus Christ from being partitioned either into two persons or into two concrete existences. It is also quite obvious, if we look at what my accusers have written, that their ideas actually agree with my own. For example, they say:

But there is absolutely no need at all to match up different verses to two different persons, or to two concrete existences, or two sons, which would mean dividing up the union, the single Son. Whatever sort of argument or methodology you use, the perfect union simply cannot be divided, nor can the single Son. Now because we have held onto this perfect union by agreeing to the formula of one Son and Christ and Lord, everything that is said about him must be taken as being said about this one, individual Son. So it is the significance of the united natures that makes it appropriate to predicate all these expressions of the Son.[53]

Right then, now that the union has been completely secured, what loophole is left, or what imaginary sort of division is there that could still be brought into the equation? Surely anyone who now at this point still dares to make distinctions would be veering right off the highway and giving up on orthodoxy altogether! How does the anathema put it? If any partition the expressions in this sort of way, so as to attribute some of them to a man who is thought of individually alongside the Word from God, and then think of others as being appropriate only to the Word of God, let them be anathema. Now, if dividing and splitting up the expressions, some of them to a man as one separate individual and others to God the Word as another separate individual, does not in reality imply a partitioning of the single Christ, or talking of two sons, then those critics of ours are indeed our opponents. But if to speak in this way does entail slicing him up, then how can they possibly criticize what we have said, given that they have themselves explicitly agreed that Emmanuel exists without division and is a totally and perfectly unified being? My own advice, and anyone with orthodox opin-

start of Cyril's *Second Tome against Nestorius,* and was later frequently used by the opponents of the Chalcedonian formula.

53. See above, p. 144.

ions would be with me, is that each and every expression needs to be understood appropriately, whether they are the ones that are said about Christ or the ones spoken directly by him. Some seem appropriate to divinity; others match more closely to the incarnate state. It is, however, because he is one and the same individual, at the same time both God and man, that he quite rightly says things that may be divine or may be human. But the real point is that both types must be predicated of the single Jesus Christ. We are not stripping the temple that came from the holy Virgin of its divinity, but neither are we imagining that God the Father's Word was without flesh after the indescribable union.

What shocks me is that while these busybodies are happy to examine my letters down to the finest detail (or so they reckon, anyway) and then ignore everything in them that is actually useful or important for demonstrating orthodox belief, they still launch vicious attacks on the basis of the very smallest hint of a suspicion, as they see it. And through these attacks they hope to be able to blackmail us. Let me quote what I said in my letter to Nestorius:

We do not partition our Savior's sayings in the Gospels between two concrete existences or two persons. The one and only Christ is not a duality, even if one thinks of him as having come together out of two distinct elements into an unbreakable union, in just the same way that one thinks of a man as constituted of both soul and body and yet as a single being, not a duality. But we are in the right when we maintain that both the human and the divine sayings were spoken by one subject. For when he says of himself, in a way that seems to refer to God, that "whoever has seen me has seen the Father," and "the Father and I are one,"[54] then we recognize in this his divine, indescribable nature, by which he is one with his own Father on the basis of their identity of substance, the image, the representation, and the reflection of his glory.[55] When, however, he is honoring humanity's limitations and so says to the Jews, "now you are seeking to kill me, a man who is speaking the truth to you,"[56] we still recognize that this is God the Word again, who is equal to and on a par with the Father, despite the limitations of his humanity. For we are obliged to believe that, while being God by nature, he became flesh, that is, a man whose flesh is endowed with

54. Jn 14.9; 10.30.   55. Cf. Heb 1.3.
56. Jn 8.40.

rational soul; then what reason would anyone have to be ashamed of his own words, even if they were appropriate for a man? For if he were to refuse to say things that are appropriate for a man, then who was making him become a man like us anyway? If he willingly demeaned himself into this self-negation for our sakes, why would he refuse to say things that are appropriate to that self-negation? So, then, all the expressions in the Gospels must be predicated of a single person, the one en-fleshed concrete existence of the Word, for the Scriptures say that there is "one Lord Jesus Christ."[57]

So, given what we have said already, there is no way we are going to be trapped being unsure about which aspect is appropriate for each saying, and there is also no way that we are going to allow these worldly and unspiritual types[58] to think in terms of two sons as a result of dividing up the concrete existences after the unfathomable union, or even to speak in such a way.

Since, however, at the beginning of their critique they cited a tiny fragment of my letter and threatened to censure us on the spur of the moment for having grievously sinned against the Word of God the Father, specifically for ill-advisedly attributing progress and growth to his own nature, something that is really appropriate only to the flesh, let us go on and say what really needs to be said by citing the whole passage from my letter. For they are frightened of the actual truth and are deceiving their audience by quoting only a part, and that is the part that seems most apt to enable them to misrepresent us in a way that makes them out to be quite reasonable. What I actually said was,

[E]ven when you hear that "Jesus advanced in age and wisdom and grace,"[59] you should not think that it follows that God's Word progressed towards being wise. Instead, recall what God's mouthpiece Paul wrote, "Christ the power of God and the wisdom of God."[60] Nor should you be so rash as to suggest, unthinkingly, that this increase in age, wisdom, and grace is simply attributable to the man. My own judgment would be that that would be exactly the same thing as dividing the single Christ into two. But then, as I have just said, the Son who existed before the ages is said to have been "appointed Son of God"[61] in the latter days of the age because, on account of the plan of salvation, he identified with his own flesh's birth. This is how he can be "his Fa-

57. 1 Cor 8.6. Extract is from Cyril's *Ep.* 17.8 (*Third Letter to Nestorius*).
58. Cf. Jude 19.   59. Lk 2.52.
60. 1 Cor 1.24.   61. Rom 1.4.

ther's wisdom" while also being said to "advance in wisdom." Although as God he remains all-perfect, he rightly took human properties upon himself so as to achieve the most complete union imaginable.[62]

Why is it that, whereas God says, "judge with a just judgment,"[63] they reason against the truth? For we neither insist on separating the concrete existences after the union nor suggest that the divine nature was in need of any progress or growth. What we do affirm, however, is that, because the Scriptures say that he became flesh, he made the properties of the flesh his own because he identified with them as part of the plan of salvation.

I will try to show that the assembly of the holy Fathers agrees with this expression of the faith and with these judgments. In order to make this totally certain I will quote a part of the explanation that was made some time ago by Atticus of blessed memory:

Today the Lord Christ submitted to the birth that brings mercy to man; he put it in the forefront, even ahead of his divine honor.[64]

In addition, he goes on to say:

Out of love for man, the Word became nothing, although he was not nothing in his own nature; for, "he emptied himself and took upon himself the form of a servant."[65] The fleshless became flesh for your sake, since "the Word became flesh."[66] He who had never been touched because his nature was not physical, was. He who had no beginning submitted to a physical beginning; he who was complete grew. The unchangeable progressed. He who was rich came into being in an inn. He who encircles heaven with clouds was swaddled. The king was placed in a manger.

When we read these following explanations from Julius and Felix, who were the leaders of the Roman church during that

62. Cyril, *Paschal Letter* 17.3.65–79, SC 372, p. 278. Also FOTC 127, p. 67.
63. Zec 7.9.
64. "Some time ago" refers to the era of the Council of Nicaea. The citations from Atticus of Constantinople, like most other patristic citations used here by Cyril, were also incorporated into the official anthology of quotations in the official records of the Council of Ephesus.
65. Phil 2.7.
66. Jn 1.14.

period, we came to appreciate that to divide up the concrete existences after union is not some harmless activity but actually entails completely reversing the holy mystery of the Incarnation.

From Julius, bishop of Rome:[67]

God's Son is proclaimed as being incarnate of the Virgin Mary so as to make our faith complete. He made his dwelling among men. He was not acting inside a man (this is how it is in the case of prophets and apostles), but was both perfect God in flesh and perfect man in spirit; not two sons, where one was the real son who took the man to himself while the other was a mortal man taken up by God; rather, a single Only-Begotten in heaven, and also upon earth the Only-Begotten God.

From Felix, the holy bishop and martyr of Rome:

Concerning the Word's Incarnation, and our faith, we believe in the Lord Jesus Christ, who was born of the Virgin Mary, that he is the eternal Son and Word of God and not a man who was taken up by God, in such a way that the latter might be another subject alongside the former. God's Son did not take to himself a man in this way, but, while being perfect God, he became at the same time also a perfect man, incarnate of the Virgin.

ϨѺ Seventh Anathema

If any say that Jesus's actions were carried out by God the Word as a man's would be,[68] and that he was endowed with the glory of the Only-Begotten as if he were another individual with a separate existence, let them be anathema.

The Orientals' Critique

No one would admit that our Lord Jesus Christ was controlled by the Spirit as a mere man, prophet, or apostle would be. On the other hand, we are not going to deny or do away with those apostolic expressions about him that take account of his visible

67. Julius and Felix were active popes from the period of the "Nicene Fathers" in the middle years of the fourth century. The following citations were commonly attributed to them as paragons of orthodoxy, although their real provenance was the erstwhile heretic Apollinarius.

68. See n. 58, p. 111, in the defense against Theodoret, above in this volume.

fleshly nature, such as, "according to that control of his mighty power which he exercised in Christ when he raised him from the dead," and, "whom God raised up, having loosed the pains of death," and, "raised up by the power of God," and so forth.[69] Now, even though these things are said with reference to what is visible, no one would thereby believe him to be a mere man who is being controlled, nor to be simply a righteous man, or a prophet or apostle. So we are not going to do away with or deny those expressions that denote his divinity, but neither are we going to start blasphemously throwing anathemas against what was also said about his visible, fleshly nature. At the same time we are not saying that he was controlled as a mere man or a righteous man would be, or a prophet or apostle. After all, he did not use the expression, "thus says the Lord," but because he was the Son and the Lawmaker he said, "I myself tell you."

Cyril's Defense

So now we are just going to use exactly the same arguments in our defense as we did before. We all agree that there is a single Lord Jesus Christ, that we believe in a single individual who is both the eternal and pre-existing Word of God the Father and who became a man in this latter part of the age, miraculously born of a woman in the flesh. Because he was a single Son, God, and Lord, he performed miracles by his superhuman strength, which assuredly proves that, even though he became flesh, he was still absolutely God, and the power of the Father. When he became a man, he did not stop being what he had been before. So when he accomplished his miracles, such as rebuking demons, crushing Satan, bringing sight to the blind, raising the dead, commanding the raging sea with a word, he was not being exalted as a man might, like some other separate Christ, as if he were nothing but a holy prophet or an apostle. No, it was for himself that he obtained his glory, so that from whatever

---

69. Eph 1.19–20; Acts 2.24; 2.33. In the last quotation, Andrew has substituted "power" for "right hand," a variant that does rather support his argument about the biblical language of the Father's power at work within the Son. It is, however, an otherwise unknown variant.

angle you look at it, even though he had become a man, people would believe that he is really God by nature. That is why it is wholly absurd to allow Nestorius to say things such as:

The activities of the Trinity are held in common and are also distinguished among the separate concrete existences. The glory of the Only-Begotten was attached at one time to the Father, at another time to the Spirit, and at another time to the power of Christ.[70]

So these folk who want to criticize us must prove that "Christ" is a different being, someone who is a separate individual, and is understood as such, someone to whom the Only-Begotten Word of God attached his power because he was really a different and individual son besides himself. Otherwise, if it is not a case of one individual here and another there, but is rather a case of their being one and the same, that is, the Only-Begotten who came from the Father and a man who in his flesh came from the Virgin, then surely they are under an obligation not merely to keep quiet but actually to wield the power of the truth as a bulwark against Nestorius's stammerings, which are nothing but baubles beside the jewel of orthodox doctrine.

So the Son was, and is, God; since at that time he donned humanity's finiteness, he made the plan of salvation effective and willingly endured everything for us by making himself nothing. This is why one may say that the Father brought him to life, even though he was really himself Life by nature; and one may say that he received glory, even though he was himself the Lord of glory. And so that Hebrew of Hebrews, the true lawgiver from the tribe of Benjamin, wrote, "Paul, an apostle sent not by men nor through a man, but through Jesus Christ and through God the Father who raised him from the dead,"[71] and who gave him glory. To balance this, although one may say that he received glory from the Father, which might be taken to entail the finiteness of being human, he was aware that, insofar as he is under-

70. This quotation comes from another of Nestorius's sermons and was again used by Cyril in the documentation at Ephesus. Loofs, *Nestoriana*, 225,13–18. Its reference to the way that the Only-Begotten's glory at one time belonged to Christ's power may have been the motivation for Cyril's seventh anathema in the first place.

71. Gal 1.1.

stood to be, and indeed is, God, he possessed a glory above that
of created things. He said, "Everything has been given to me by
my Father," and, "No one but the Father knows who the Son
is, nor does anyone know who the Father is but the Son and
those to whom the Son reveals it."[72] Maybe one of those aca-
demic types will say: if everything has been given to you by your
Father because you lacked glory and if you needed to have infinite power bestowed upon you because you are human, then
how can you go on and say that it is impossible for anyone to
know you merely with their human understanding in just the
same way as one cannot know the Father? Quite right, he would
reply; in terms of what you can see, knowledge about me is not
veiled, for I am God in flesh and blood, and one may know me
in terms of my flesh, but in terms of my actual divine nature
and glory I am God's equal and I transcend all understanding
and every description. So, then, we will hold onto what has been
prescribed and will not deny the apostolic sayings, God forbid!
Neither would we oppose descriptions of the Incarnation by either thinking or saying anything unreasonable. Instead we consistently follow the Holy Scriptures and treat what the Fathers
have said with the greatest importance. We only oppose people
who are perverting the church's orthodox doctrines.

No one would doubt that when it says that the Father raised
our Lord Jesus Christ from the dead, this refers to him acting
specifically upon the flesh. But he himself is the life-giver and
God's active power, who gave life to his own temple and said,
"Destroy this temple, and I will raise it up again in three days."[73]
So, then, this body to which he imparted life was not a different
thing, nor did it belong to some other man like us. It was the
Word's very own.

?❧ Eighth Anathema

If any dare to say that the man who was taken up should be
worshiped, glorified, and named together with God the Word,
as if they were two separate individuals, rather than honoring

72. Mt 11.27.
73. Jn 2.19.

Emmanuel with a single act of worship and ascribing to him a single act of praise, seeing that the Word became flesh, let them be anathema.

The Orientals' Critique

We would not say that they are to be worshiped "together" or glorified "together" as if there were two persons, concrete existences, or sons, or as if our worship were to be given to the flesh and to God the Word separately. No, we would offer a single act of worship, and so forth, to one Son. One may then add the term "together," as Cyril himself does in his first treatise:

You see, although in his role as the Word he continued to sit together with his own Father, and although his existence by nature depended upon him and remained within him, he still listened, with his flesh, to the words, "Sit at my right hand until I make your enemies a footstool for your feet."[74] That is the way in which we reckon that we, and the holy angels too, should worship him.[75]

It should be added that Cyril is being excessively pedantic when he denounces those who wish to worship the single individual Son "together with" his flesh, as if this phrase "together with" meant anything different from the word "with," which is the word he himself used in the above quotation when he said that the Son ought to be worshiped "with" his flesh, while at the same time denying that the flesh should be worshiped "together with" the divinity.

---

74. Ps 110.1 (109.1 LXX), though Andrew is thinking of New Testament uses of this verse in reference to the incarnate Christ, such as Mt 22.44 and especially Heb 1.13.

75. Cyril, *Paschal Letter* 17.2.90–96, SC 372, p. 266. See also FOTC 127, p. 62. It was this letter that sparked the controversy with Nestorius. (Andrew refers to it as "the first treatise," which is also how he referred to a quotation from the *Letter to the Monks,* above.) "Together with": The Greek compound element *sun-,* which may be added to verbs such as "to worship" or "to glorify," was rejected as a Nestorian invention by Cyril; but his critic here finds an instance in his own writings in which he encouraged the worship of the Son "with" (*meta*) his flesh. The argument here is that the two terms cannot mean anything different and so Cyril is again contradicting himself.

Cyril's Defense

God's mouthpiece Paul spoke with great insight when he said, "Examine yourselves to see whether you are still in the faith."[76] You see, whenever the human mind veers off the highway or shifts its position away from orthodox thinking, then its love of itself tends to make it wary and fearful of ever calling its own ideas false. But it may very easily correct itself by attending carefully to the hard work that was exerted by those holy Fathers who are justly and universally renowned for the orthodoxy and precision of their doctrine, and then by carefully testing one's own faith against theirs. Anyone with common sense would be sure to follow their judgments, because they also filled their own minds with the apostolic and evangelical tradition and based their own theological writings purely and flawlessly upon the Holy Scriptures. They were "stars in the universe, holding out the word of life,"[77] as the Scripture puts it. So, our father and bishop Athanasius, who is held in such very high regard, wrote as follows on the subject of our universal Savior Christ:

We confess that he is the Son of God and God in the Spirit, and man in the flesh. We do not confess that this single Son is two natures, one to be worshiped and one not to be worshiped. He is rather one incarnate nature of the Word, and is to be worshiped, with his flesh, with a single worship. There are not two sons, one the true Son of God who is worshiped, and the other a man from Mary who is not worshiped, but who has become a son of God by grace in the way that men do.[78]

And again a little further on:

So the one who is begotten of the Virgin Mary is God's Son and is genuinely God by nature, not simply by grace or a sharing of essence. In his flesh alone he is a man from Mary, but in the Spirit he is himself God's Son and God.[79]

---

76. 2 Cor 13.5.   77. Phil 2.15–16.

78. This citation was one of those later identified by Leontius of Jerusalem (*Against the Monophysites,* ed. Gray, p. 121) as being actually from the pen of Apollinarius (see Lietzmann, *Apollinaris,* 119–21, 146–47, 250). It included the famous expression "one incarnate nature of the Word," which, although for Cyril it summed up orthodox Christology, became a bone of contention once its "heretical" origins had been demonstrated.

79. Lietzmann, *Apollinaris,* 251,12–15.

And again:

If anyone teaches anything beyond what comes from the Holy Scriptures by talking of the Son of God and then of another one who is from
Mary, one who is adopted by grace as we are; if they talk about two
sons, one who is in his nature the Son of God who is from God, and the
other a man from Mary who is Son by grace; or if someone says that the
flesh of our Lord is from heaven and not from the Virgin Mary, or that
the divinity was turned into flesh, or was confused with it, or was altered into it, or that the Lord's divinity could suffer, or that our Lord's
flesh should not be worshiped because it is a man's and not the Lord
our God's, such a person the holy and catholic church anathematizes
under the impulse of the inspired apostle who said, "If any preach to
you something beyond what you received, let them be anathema."[80]

Even though Athanasius had advisedly written all this, that
man Nestorius chose to attack Christ's glory and gave free rein
to his unguarded tongue on the same subject. There is one
place where he says this:

We would confess God in a man; we would pay reverence to a man
who is worshiped together with God by being connected with God the
Word.[81]

Is he not very obviously calling Christ a god-bearing man and
saying that a man was simply connected with God, perhaps on
the basis of something that Paul once said: "He who is joined to
the Lord is one spirit with him"?[82] But surely it is more accurate
to say that the same individual is at the same time both God
and man rather than, as some man understood, to be a separate
individual who has a contingent connection with God. Conse-
quently, after the inexpressible union, even if someone were to
call Emmanuel God, the Word of God ought to be understood
as in a state of being made man and being incarnate. Even when
we call him a man, we know that he is also the Word of the Father himself. It is, therefore, one thing to say that the Word of
God the Father is one Son even after the flesh had been united
to him, and quite another to say that God was "in a man," which

80. Gal 1.9. The entire extract is from Lietzmann, *Apollinaris*, 253,3–14.

81. Loofs, *Nestoriana,* 249,2–4, although the citation there is taken from
another slightly different version found in the second of Cyril's *Tomes against
Nestorius.*

82. 1 Cor 6.17.

is really no different from how he was in the prophets, or even in us ourselves, by means of the Holy Spirit. If you want to be quite safe and avoid any criticism, then I would advise you to say that the incarnate Word of God, because he exists as a single Son, is not something other than his own flesh, but rather that he should be worshiped with it—somewhat like the way in which a man's soul is honored with his own body; he is denoted by a single name because, like a creature, he is constituted out of those two elements. So then, how could anyone bear it or pass over such an obvious insult in silence when, because you are so keen to discuss Christ our universal Savior, you end up dividing what is single into two and you pronounce that there is a man understood as a separate individual, and then are even so bold as to suggest that one must worship this man together with God, that they should share the name of God, as if he who is Son of God by nature were another Christ besides him? You ought rather to have said: "We would pay reverence to the Word of God, who has become a man and is called God and is worshiped in this humanity because he is also God by nature and made visible from God the Father."

"But look here," my opponents shout, "we have caught him writing in his own letter that the Son sits together with his Father even with his own flesh. How can that be any different from saying that the man is to be worshiped together with God the Word and given the name of God in common with him? For the expressions 'together with' and 'with' mean just the same thing." Well, my riposte would be that they have no idea about the meanings of these words and no grasp on the real issues that are at stake here. When the discussion has considered closely what elements have come together to become, or to compose, the single person and nature, or concrete existence, then it may use either of the terms, "together with" or "with," because it has already secured what it denotes and has thereby defined it as a single composite entity rather than dividing it into a duality. But once the concrete existences have already been split into two, and then, as well as understanding each of them as a separate individual, one goes on to use these expressions, "together with" or "with," then they would in effect indicate at least two entities, if not more, rather than a single composite entity. It would be like saying that a man's soul is to be honored "together with his own body," if some of its honor belonged to the one man, who derives from both elements; that is, if someone were to say that his soul is a single creature "with his body," then he would not thereby be dividing the single man into a duality in any way at all. On the contrary, he would be demonstrating that he knew full well which elements he was derived from, or which composed his nature. When, for instance, you say, "Peter is designated as a man together with John," or that "John went up to the temple with Peter," you are not using terms such as "together with" or "with" to denote a single entity, since Peter and John are not a composite entity and the pair of them do not go to make up a single man. Why, then, are they so playing around with the truth by dividing the single Christ into two? If they reckon that to say that "the Son sat together with his Father along with his own flesh" leaves room to be interpreted as meaning two sons, then let them ask whether we are saying that the one Son is honored with a single "sitting together" or with two, one for the body alone and the other for the Word. But they cannot show this to be the case. How so? Because we would insist that the Son, who is one with his own flesh, is a single individual, at the same time both God and man, who is honored with a single "sitting together" with his Father. But then to say that the man is worshiped together with God and that they are together given the name of God is really tantamount to admitting that there are two objects of worship and two beings who share a name with each other. Any such argument is both simplistic and at some distance from being accurate or orthodox, and that is why I wrote this anathema, which is directed against people who in any way divide Emmanuel into a man and God the Word as individuals. Both the writings of the Fathers and the genuine interpretation of the Holy Scriptures declare to us that he is one.

৯ৠ *Ninth Anathema*

If any suggest that the one Lord Jesus Christ was glorified by the Spirit by making use of a power that came through the Spirit, a power that was something other than his own, and that he received from the Spirit the ability to overcome evil spirits and perform divine miracles for people, instead of saying that the Spirit by which he wrought the miracles was his very own, let them be anathema.

The Orientals' Critique

Once again it will be appropriate to make a note of something he has said once before and to point out that he seems to have forgotten what he himself has written. He proved not just that the Lord performed his miracles in the Spirit, but that he was also raised from the dead in the Spirit. In his first treatise he wrote as follows:

If then he did not experience death in the flesh, as the Scriptures say, then neither was he raised to life in the Spirit.[83]

We need, then, to take a closer look at this self-contradiction, because in this anathema he denies that the Lord expelled demons and performed miracles by the Spirit of God and he ignores what the Lord expressly says in the Gospels, that "if by the Spirit of God I cast out demons."[84] We, in contrast, confess that our Lord Jesus Christ accomplished the miracles both by his own power and by the Spirit's activity. He did not make use of the Spirit's power because he did not have any of his own. To deny that the Holy Spirit was present at the same time is tantamount, I would say, to a denial of the Holy Scriptures, because even when it says that the Father performed miraculous deeds, it is still the Son who is doing it, as in the verse "The Father remains in me, and he performs the deeds which I do."[85] After all, everything that belongs to the Father belongs to the Son. So even when it says that the Spirit did it, as in the verse "if by the Spirit of God I cast out demons," it is still the Lord who is doing it, in the Spirit. The Son is not something foreign to the Father and the Spirit, and the activities of the Trinity are neither separate nor individual. Rather, any activity that is de-

83. *Ep.* 1 (*To the Monks*) 25.   84. Mt 12.28.
85. Jn 14.10, 12.

scribed in the Scripture as belonging to one of the concrete existences belongs to the Trinity as a whole. For instance, there is one place where Scripture says first that the whole of creation is the Son's doing: "By the Word of the Lord were the heavens established," and then that it is the Spirit's: "and all their host by the Spirit of his mouth."[86] It obviously was not because the Father was incapable that the Son acted to create the world, nor was it because the Son was too weak to create that the Spirit helped out (it does say, after all, that "all things were created through him").[87] The reason why the Scripture predicates the very same things sometimes of the Father, sometimes of the Son, and sometimes of the Spirit, is to commend to us the doctrine that the members of the Trinity are equal in substance, in honor, and in power. We thus understand everything to depend upon a single divine substance, out of which the Only-Begotten was born, without experiencing suffering, seeing as he was the Word who has a real and substantial existence.[88] The Spirit, too, itself proceeds from that substance and exists in its own individual concrete existence, since the single substance leaves its mark on each of the three concrete existences. No one of them can be understood as being something different from what that substance really is,[89] but each is distinguished from the others in terms of its own characteristic, definable properties. When there is but a single substance, a single power, and a single will, how can there possibly be individual activities? All these things are held in common, and so there is definitely only one activity.

Cyril's Defense

Do I really need to bring forward evidence to prove that my opponents are willing to write meaningless rubbish and that they are prepared to insult us most unadvisedly? Yet their own

86. Ps 33.6 (32.6 LXX). Normally, "breath of his mouth," but the translation "Spirit" makes the argument clearer in this case.

87. Jn 1.3.

88. "real and substantial existence": *enousios kai enupostatos.*

89. "what that substance really is": *logos tês ousias,* an expression taken from the opening to Aristotle's *Categories.*

argument, I would say, proves my point all by itself. What we clearly maintained in this anathema was that the Holy Spirit belonged to the Son and performed miracles through him. Yet, despite the fact that they keep on insisting that I have forgotten what I said, they have become so crass as actually to believe that I said that it was not by means of the Spirit that Jesus expelled the demons! How dishonest is that! If they really do not think that expelling demons counts as a miracle, then they can say whatever they want! Let them initiate a prosecution against me! Let them charge me with not making this clear enough and not mentioning miracles at all. But if expelling demons is actually just as much of an astonishing miracle as any of the others, then why do they reject a perfectly good way of speaking as useless and run away from the obligation to speak accurately as if it were something rotten? Why do they set so much store on the gibberish they throw at us and yet deem of very little interest something that is universally condemned by God and man? I reckon they have forgotten the time when Christ said, "How can you say to your brother, 'Brother, let me take the speck out of your eye,' when all the time there is a plank in your own eye? Hypocrite! First take the plank out of your own eye, and then you will see clearly to remove the speck from your brother's eye."[90]

It is not from their arguments that we have learned that the Holy Trinity is consubstantial, equal in power and activity. It was the Holy Scriptures that made us certain of this. It is perfectly straightforward to see that this anathema in no way undermines the arguments for orthodox doctrine; rather, it upholds them. The anathema is designed to prevent people from dividing up the one Lord Jesus Christ and splitting him into a man and God the Word as separate individuals, as we have been pointing out constantly, as if he could be understood as being two persons or concrete existences severed from one another. It also prevents people from saying that, in order to have performed his miracles, Jesus must have been controlled by the activity of the Spirit as a normal man might be. This would make him no different from those holy apostles and prophets who through heaven's

90. Mt 7.4–5.

mercy were filled with divine gifts and were able to say, "By the grace of God we are what we are."[91] To say such a thing as this is perfectly apt for a holy man, who has received a notable portion of God's gifts, but not at all for Christ. For the Holy Spirit is his very own, just as, of course, it is also the Father's own. He acts by means of the Spirit in just the way that the Father also does. Furthermore, even though he said to the Jews, "I have shown you many good works from the Father," and, "I do not speak on my own authority; but the Father lives in me, and he accomplishes the deeds," and, "if by the Spirit of God I cast out demons,"[92] he attributes the activity done through the Spirit both to himself and to the Father because they all share in the one substance. Now a great deal more could be said on this subject, but I think the time has come to broaden our discussion, if you are willing to follow. We would not, then, say that Emmanuel was controlled by the Spirit as by some power other than himself. Rather, he made use of it by his divine status and possessed as his very own the power of the Spirit, which was consubstantial with him. When the blessed disciples performed miracles, they said, "My friends, why do you stare at us as if by our own power or godliness we had made this lame man who sits by the Beautiful Gate walk?[93] Christ's Spirit belongs to him!" Well then, this is what I say to those who are trying to satirize what we have written: if it is part of their whole purpose to partition what cannot be partitioned and to say that Jesus was controlled by the Spirit as a normal man would be, then there is not much more to be said about people who are so disposed; but if they do agree that there is a single Christ, Son, and Lord, that the same individual is at the same time both God and man, then like us they ought to believe that he was not controlled by a power that was better than he or different from him, but that it was he himself who enacted the miracles by means of his own Spirit, which has the power to do anything. Enough now of these pointless tirades and jealous outbursts.

91. 1 Cor 15.10.   92. Jn 10.32; 14.10; Mt 12.28.
93. Acts 3.12.

✨ *Tenth Anathema*

Divine Scripture says that Christ became "the high priest and apostle of our confession"[94] and that he "offered himself for us as a sweet-smelling savor to God the Father."[95] Therefore, if any say that it was not the Word of God himself who became our high priest and apostle when he became incarnate and a man like us, but another, separate individual besides him, one born from a woman, or if any say that he brought this offering on his own behalf rather than just on our behalf (for the one who knew no sin was not in need of any offering), let them be anathema.

The Orientals' Critique

If God the Word is a high priest, then who was his God? To what sort of deity can he have brought his offerings? He has forgotten that the blessed Paul wrote, "We do not have a high priest who is unable to sympathize with our weaknesses, but one who was tempted in every way, though without sinning."[96] Who is this who was tempted? Was it God the Word, or was it the human nature, David's seed? Once more, "No one takes the honor upon himself; rather, he is called to it by God, just as Aaron was. In the same way, Christ did not take on himself the glory of becoming a high priest."[97] Who is this who is compared directly, in terms of his priestly honor, with Aaron himself, with someone who did not take that honor upon himself, but was called to it by God, and who was raised up to priestly honor? Is it really the divine nature that is co-eternal with the Father and which possesses all that the Father does as its own? What sort of honor could he have been raised to that was higher than what he already had? Shall we really say that the priesthood is a more honorable thing than the divine nature, and that he ascended to it not by himself but only through God's calling him there, and that he was then glorified through it? Or was this David's seed, which came into

---

94. Heb 3.1.
96. Heb 4.15.

95. Eph 5.2.
97. Heb 5.4, 5.

being and was set apart, and to which, through the psalmist, God swore that the priesthood should be given in eternity? What he swore was, "The Lord will not change his mind; you are a priest forever, in the order of Melchizedek."[98] Was it really the divinity of the Only-Begotten that accepted these oaths from God that he would receive an eternal priesthood and be glorified through that? Which of us could bear to say, or even think, such a thing? Who would not condemn us if we suggested that God was appointed high priest and had received those sworn promises, that he was called to that priestly honor rather than receiving it by right, and that he was to be compared to the man who was the first to receive it? Again, it says, "He says in another place, 'You are a priest forever, in the order of Melchizedek.'"[99] Who is this whose order of priesthood is compared to that of Melchizedek? Is it really right to think that it is God the Word or the human flesh that he took and which was united to him without division or confusion? It goes on to say, "During the days of his flesh, he offered up prayers and petitions with fervent cries and tears to the one who could save him from death."[100] Was it really God the Word who offered up prayers and petitions with fervent cries and tears to the one who could save him, and who "was heard because of his piety and learned obedience from what he suffered"?[101] Well, if this high priest is God the Word, then it follows that he himself "learned from what he suffered and was made perfect."[102] But do not let yourself be worried when you hear about the one who suffers, "even though he was Son."[103] There is no need for us to talk of two sons, one who suffered and another who remained without suffering, nor is he who is from David's seed given the name of "Son" separately from the divinity or on his own account, as if the divinity were himself no longer called "Son" after the union apart from his visible flesh. After the union, the sonship is one with both the natures, because they are not separated from each other; in fact, after the union, there is no separation at all; the unity lasts forever. Even when it comes to suffering, the divinity cannot be separated

98. Ps 110.4 (109.4 LXX).   99. Heb 5.6.
100. Heb 5.7.   101. Heb 5.7–8.
102. Heb 5.8–9.   103. Heb 5.8.

from its flesh, even though the former is impassible, and those things that pertained to divinity were made perfect through the flesh. That is why we can acknowledge a single individual to be one and the same Son, even though the natures remain unconfused. We do not talk about one individual and then another (God forbid!) but only of one and the same individual. Everyone will happily agree that the Holy Scriptures say that our Lord Jesus Christ became our high priest and apostle, but not that the man who is of a woman was a separate individual from the Word of God the Father. We can then say that it is because the one who is of David's seed was inexpressibly united, without confusion or division, to the Word of God, that, in his role as high priest, he could be tempted in every way, yet without sinning, and learn obedience from what he suffered, and that his very own flesh could bring offerings to God the Father on our behalf only, not for himself too. It would be inadvisable for us to say that God the Word was a high priest or that he himself brought offerings to God the Father, for God is not the Father of the Only-Begotten One's divinity, but simply Father.

Cyril's Defense

This is the moment when we ought to ask our adversaries, "How long will you waver between two poles?"[104] It is high time you developed a more appropriate and exacting attitude towards the real science of theology, rather than being handicapped by your wavering ideas, your diseased mind, and your unwillingness simply to walk in a straight line! Those who have wavering ideas are unstable in all they do, and they do not receive anything from the Lord.[105] And I say this while I am still somewhat in shock at just how readily and viciously they are prepared to attack this anathema that we are now discussing. It is not at all surprising that they should be wary of our using the title "apostle and high priest of our confession" in reference to the Word of God the Father, even after he had become a man. After all, anyone who tries to belittle his nativity in the flesh or who dares to cast it aside,

104. 1 Kgs 18.21. See n. 80 at *Against Theodoret* 9, p. 118, above.
105. Cf. Jas 1.7–8.

as though it were not genuine, and who avoids calling the holy Virgin "Mother-of-God," is bound to miss out on various aspects of the salvation plan. We should take heed to what Isaiah said: "If you will not have faith, then neither will you understand."[106] When he said that the Word had become flesh, John the evangelist, who is God's mouthpiece, was speaking words that struck the earth like the most massive thunderbolt. Only those who disregard the real meaning of these words would say that it means that he became flesh in the sense of becoming a sin and a curse.[107] We already discussed this particular topic earlier and said there all we needed to prove their arguments wholly facile. To those who are pressing us on this, all that we need add for the moment is this: just accept the basic mystery of Christ, the fundamental principle and, so to speak, the starting point of the plan of salvation; have faith in the Holy Scriptures, as we do; accept the decree of truth and agree that the Only-Begotten Word of God, who is in the Father's bosom, through whom and in whom are all things, became flesh, not after experiencing a change of mixing, but remaining always what he naturally is, was, and shall be. He became flesh after experiencing birth from the holy Virgin (in the flesh, I would add), he was called the Son of Man, and he partook of blood and flesh for our sakes. To people who are confident of this and who accept this faith as sacred and genuine, everything becomes totally transparent and straightforward rather than an uphill struggle. As it is written, "All things are clear to those who understand, and right to those who find knowledge."[108]

It is now the moment to explain how this anathema arose. That Nestorius, who is always mixed-up and turns things completely on their heads, said the following about our universal Savior Jesus Christ:

He was sent to preach repentance to the captives: this is the man who was made a faithful high priest toward God (for he came into existence, not pre-existing eternally). This was the man—you heretic!—who progressed little by little towards the dignity of high priesthood.[109]

---

106. Is 7.9 LXX.

107. See the discussion of the first anathema. Scriptural allusions are to Gal 3.13 and 2 Cor 5.21.

108. Prv 8.9.   109. Pusey, *Tomes*, p. 99.

He goes on to add other things besides this, which give birth to comparable profanities. On hearing such outrageous expressions, who would not prefer to go through any trials rather than prefer to remain silent, which would be so abhorrent to God? Christ died for us; he scorned shame and endured the cross[110] and death in the flesh. Should we not repay our benefactor with the service of speaking out? Or do we just sit back quietly while we listen to such crazy calumnies? Or even partake in these accusations that he so wantonly waffles on about? What on earth are you suggesting? That he only became high priest little by little? Even though he who was God the Word emptied himself, even though he who was naturally free took upon himself the form of a servant, even though he who was superior to all coming-into-existence and who exulted in his divine transcendence humbled himself! If he "progressed," in what sense could he have emptied himself? How could he have come down to this low state? Who would suggest that this self-emptying was the thing that first introduced him to glory and honor? What would be the point of his emptying himself in that case?

But then, they say, if the very Word of God the Father became a high priest, who is the one that is greater than he, the one whom he is attending to by his priestly service? Then I simply say yet again, have faith that, even though the Son is naturally divine and in the form of the Father, he "did not intend to grasp at equality with God; instead he emptied himself by taking the form of a servant."[111] If he did indeed become a man and took upon himself the form of a servant, then how could one reckon that being called "apostle and high priest" is at all insignificant or ill-suited to expressions about the plan of salvation? How could he who did not scorn our human limitations have considered human things as so much garbage to be cast aside? I suppose it would be quite easy to say lots more and to extend this discussion much further. But leaving that option aside for now, I would rather bring some further quotations from what these individuals have written:

110. Cf. Heb 12.2.
111. Phil 2.7.

There is no need for us to talk of two sons, one who suffered and another who remained without suffering, nor is he who is from David's seed given the name of "son" separately from the divinity or on his own account, as if the divinity were himself no longer called "son" after the union apart from his visible flesh.[112]

And then also:

That is why we can acknowledge a single individual to be one and the same Son, even though the natures remain unconfused. We do not talk about one individual and then another (God forbid!) but only of one and the same individual. Everyone will happily agree that the Holy Scriptures say that our Lord Jesus Christ became our high priest and apostle, but not that the man who is of a woman was a separate individual from the Word of God the Father.

So then, if, as they put it, there is a single Son, and if they do not at all divide him into two sons (one being from David's seed, the other the Word of God the Father), how are they not still undermining the mystery by partitioning the plan of salvation between man and God, since all things, whether human or divine, belong to him? You see, when someone says something about him that is especially fitting for a god, we say that it is absolutely correct, since we know that he is God, and if what is said is something more appropriate to a human, we would also assent. For we confess that God exists in flesh and blood, and we recognize, through these human things, the limitations of humanity. Thousands upon thousands of holy angels are serving him, and the seraphim are standing around his divine throne.[113] When he became a man, he was given the title of high priest, not in the sense that he was offering his sacrifice to a god greater than he, but so as to procure our confession of faith both in himself and in the Father. You are ashamed when you hear that he was given the title of high priest for humanity's sake. So why are you not amazed when I say that the type of sacrifice he made was not the usual one for priests but was rather made for himself and for the Father? I would agree with you when you say that making sacrifices is not a suitable activity for God, but that is an accurate thing to say only if the Word

112. See the Orientals' critique above for both these quotations.
113. Cf. Dn 7.10; Is 6.2.

was separate from the flesh. When he became human, however, look at how he makes sacrifice on behalf of humanity and also, as God, with transcendent honors, since he is enthroned next to God the Father. Look at how he both makes sacrifice at the human level and yet is enthroned as God. What did the blessed Paul say? "We do have such a high priest who sat down at the right hand of the throne of the Majesty in the heavens."[114] So, seeing as he became human while being God, and that the Son is one and the same individual, we can attribute everything to this one individual. We are fully aware of the ways of the plan of salvation, and we are always exerting the full strength of our intelligence to obey him with all our sense and skill.

✌ *Eleventh Anathema*

If any do not confess that the Lord's flesh has the power to give life and that it belongs to the Word of God the Father himself, but think that it belongs to another individual besides him who is connected to him as a matter of honor or as if he were merely in possession of a divine indwelling, rather than, as we already said, that it is life-giving because it has become a property of the Word, who has the strength to give life to all, let them be anathema.

The Orientals' Critique

It is all right to confess that, because of the union, our Lord's flesh belonged personally to the Word, so long as one realizes that it was taken from us. There is no need to add that it does not "belong to another individual besides him," unless of course he is denying that the flesh was assumed from us. To repeat so frequently that the Lord's flesh is of our nature almost amounts to a denial. Where is our boasting? Who, according to Paul, "raised us up and seated us"?[115] How could anyone's flesh belong to anyone other than himself? Surely each of us has flesh that is common to everyone by reason of their consubstantiality, but

114. Heb 8.1.
115. Rom 3.27; Eph 2.6.

which is also personal insofar as the flesh of each person is not someone else's but belongs solely to him whose flesh it is. What is he trying to achieve when he says that "it belongs to him," as if it could have been someone else's? If he reckons that the Lord's flesh was taken from our own and also reckons that the flesh of each person belongs to him whose flesh it is, rather than belonging to someone else, then why does he say that it belongs to him like some foreign thing? Or is it the case that this is just a veil covering his actual denial that his flesh is taken from our own nature? He said it more clearly in his first treatise:

The baby was not like us; that is to say, he was not in our likeness in a simple and straightforward manner, yet he was among humanity on account of the flesh and he was divine insofar as he surpassed us and came from heaven.[116]

And then in the second treatise he says:

What was born from the Virgin was not the body of some other one like us; rather, it belonged to him who is the Word of the Father.[117]

Who would ever suggest that the Lord's flesh might have belonged to any other person that ever lived? Perhaps it was Abel's, or Noah's, or Elijah's, or [belonged to] some other figure from the past? Not only have we already explained that the Lord's flesh did not belong to anyone else who ever lived, but also that it belonged solely to the Lord, who was united without confusion or separation to God the Word. Moreover, as we have said, the flesh of each one of us could never come to belong to anyone other than the person whose flesh it is. Given that the entire church is in agreement with us on this point, what on earth is he trying to achieve by repeating so often that the flesh belonged to him, unless he is actually denying that the flesh is of our own nature? How can he forbid us from saying that he was connected to it as a matter of honor or power, given that in his first treatise he says:

---

116. Cyril, *Paschal Letter* 17.3.9–12, SC 372, pp. 273–74. Also FOTC 127, p. 65.

117. *Ep*.1.20 (ACO 1.1.1.20.9–11). Andrew now attributes to the "second treatise" another citation from the *Letter to the Monks*, previously cited from the "first treatise."

This is how we have been made rich by his poverty, by our human nature being raised up in him to a level of honor that is appropriate to divinity.[118]

But we would retort to him (and he is contradicting himself here), that if the natures remain unconfused, while the unity also persists, and we continue to say that worship, power, honor, and authority ought to be offered as if to a single Son, precisely because the natures remain unconfused within the union, then what else need be said to describe the union any more exactly? We would concede and agree with him, just so long as the natures are not to be confused. It seems clear that nothing will satisfy him as a way of expressing the absolute unity, for fear of confusing the natures. We, however, keep the natures quite safe from becoming confused, and we confess the most absolute divine and incomprehensible unity, while we offer all of it for the glory of both the Father and the single Son, and we say together with the blessed Peter, "You are the Christ, the Son of God."[119]

Cyril's Defense

At the time when those awful Jews, mentally wounded by the arrows of jealousy, worked themselves up into an unholy anger, and when they even tried to lay their unholy hands upon Christ (our universal Savior), he ordered them to explain why they dared to do such a thing: "I have shown you many good works from my Father. For which of these are you stoning me?" But they had got to such a point of insanity and unholy intentions that they even tried to bring him down with accusations of blasphemy, by saying, "We are not stoning you for any good work, but for blasphemy, because you, although you are a man, are making yourself out to be God." The Savior replied by saying, "Is it not written in your law, 'I have said, You are gods'? If he called 'gods' those people to whom the word of God came, and the Scripture cannot be set aside, then why are you saying that the one whom the Father sanctified and sent into the world is

---

118. Cyril, *Paschal Letter* 17.2.87–89, SC 372, p. 266. Also FOTC 127, p. 62.
119. Mt 16.16.

blaspheming, because I said that I am God's Son?"[120] We have thoroughly investigated what is meant in this passage by his "being sent," and we have collected information on this point from all over the Holy Scriptures. He himself said through Isaiah, "The Spirit of the Lord is upon me because he has anointed me to preach the good news to the poor; he has sent me to proclaim freedom for the prisoners, and to open the eyes of the blind."[121] We would argue that when the Son became a man he was "sent" by God the Father. Both the term and the reality of "mission" are especially appropriate to the limitations of the self-emptying.[122] The Word of God the Father was sent, as I have said, not naked and without flesh, but rather he experienced being born in the flesh, or taking to himself a body, from the holy Virgin. Once this body had been united to him without confusion, in some way that cannot be described, then the Lord God appeared to us according to the Scriptures. We say, therefore, that the body came to belong to the Word rather than to some man individually and separately, someone thought of as being another besides Christ the Son. We should think of it happening to Christ in just the same way that each of our bodies is said to belong individually to us. Even though it is akin to our own bodies, and consubstantial with them (since he was born of a woman), it is thought of, and spoken of, as belonging to him. Since the Word of God the Father is by nature life itself, he demonstrated that his flesh has the power to bestow life. This is just how the gift of life was bestowed upon us. And so Christ said, "I am the living bread that came down from heaven and gives life to the world," and then, "This bread that I am giving is my flesh, for the life of the world," and then, "Whoever eats my flesh and drinks my blood remains in me, and I in them."[123] See how he always refers to his own body, the one that came from a woman, because the unity was such an absolute one. Since this

120. Jn 10.32–36.

121. Is 61.1; Lk 4.18.

122. The terms here translated "sent" and "mission" are based on the same verbal root, which is central to Cyril's argument here. This is difficult to bring out in English.

123. Jn 6.51, 33, 56.

is the grounds of the mystery, Nestorius in his own explanation
of it said this:

Listen carefully to this saying and what it means: "the one who eats
my flesh." Bear in mind that he is talking about his flesh. It was not
I who called it flesh, lest I seem to my opponents to be misinterpreting it. What he said was, "the one who eats my flesh and drinks my
blood," not, "the one who eats my divinity and drinks my divinity." It
goes, "The one who eats my flesh and drinks my blood remains in me
and I in him." Bear in mind that he is talking about his flesh. "Just as
the living Father sent me," that is, "me, the visible one." But maybe
there are times when I misinterpret. Let us listen to what comes next:
"just as the living Father sent me." My opponent says that he means the
divinity; I say that he means the humanity. Let us see who it is who is
misinterpreting this expression: "just as the living Father sent me." The
heretic says that here it means the divinity, [as if it said,] "The living
Father sent me, God the Word, and I, God the Word, am alive because
of the Father." After this, "and he that eats me will live." What are we
eating, divinity or humanity?[124]

We have talked enough now about all this extraordinary nonsense of his. What he is hoping to achieve by denying that God
the Word, incarnate and made man, was sent, while also asserting (as he says) that the visible person was a separate individual, I can hardly say, though his trick of logic is patent enough.
He completely does away with the notion of the union so as to
conclude that Christ's body is just a common human one rather than belonging personally to the one who has the power to
bestow life. Admittedly everything at the human level is insignificant to God the Word, but since he was reckoned worthy
to experience self-emptying for the world's deliverance, even
though he is said to have been sent to proclaim freedom for
prisoners and to open the eyes of the blind, still he is glorified
for having undergone the humiliation of becoming incarnate
for salvation's sake. I do not suppose anyone in his right mind
would criticize him for bringing himself down to our level for
our own sakes. Is this not the man who, by arguing that the visible person was some other Son and Christ besides the Word of
God, to whom alone God assigned the task of mission, came up
with the doctrine of cannibalism? Is he not the one who took

124. Loofs, *Nestoriana*, 227,20–228,16.

the minds of the faithful and profanely directed them towards insipid ideas? Is he not the one who tried to subject to human logic ideas that may be grasped only by an unquestioning faith? The fact that it was not the divine nature being eaten does not entail that Christ's holy body was a common human one. But what must be realized, as we have said before, is that the body belonged especially to the Word, who makes all things live. It was able to bestow life because it was the body of a living being. This is how the Son brings life to our mortal bodies and overcomes the power of death. The Holy Spirit of Christ bestows life upon us in just the same way, for "the Spirit is life-giving," as our Savior said.[125]

It would not hurt to introduce some quotations from the holy Fathers, lest it may seem that it is only I who say that the Word's body belongs to him. Then my opponents may realize that there is no point to their tirades since I am always following what they have already said. So here is the well-known father Bishop Athanasius in his work on the subject of the Holy Trinity:

He showed that he had a body, not in appearance, but in truth. It was appropriate for the Lord, when he put on human flesh, to put it on whole, together with the sufferings proper to it; so that, just as we say that the body belonged to him himself, so we may also say that the body's sufferings belonged to him himself, even though they did not touch him as far as his divinity was concerned.[126]

And also:

We have had to examine these points so that, whenever we see him doing or saying anything divinely through the instrument of his own body, we may know that it is as God that he is doing it.[127]

That is what our blessed father Athanasius had to say. It should be added that, even though one speaks of the Word's body as belonging to him, it did still come from a woman and it is of the same sort as ours, as one would expect flesh to be. The blessed Paul says that "the first man was from the earth, the second from heaven," and Christ himself says that "no one has

125. Jn 6.63.
126. Athanasius, *Contra Arianos* 3.32.
127. Ibid. 3.35.

gone up to heaven except the one who comes down from heaven, the Son of Man."[128] I would argue, however, that the Word did not say this because he had brought down from heaven the body that was united to him. It is precisely because, despite his being from heaven above, he nonetheless made the body that was united to him (in a manner that cannot be described or understood, without any change or confusion) his very own, that he could still say that he was from heaven even after he had become a Son of Man. So, given that I am expressing myself perfectly accurately and irreproachably, how can these people who are so fond of criticizing us really use this as an opportunity for their sophistry? If the anathema is fighting a battle against certain profane formulae, then is it opposing the truth with a lie? Personally, I think it is entirely appropriate for me to say that Christ is above us, since, even when the Word of God became a man, he was nonetheless not so only above us, but was also over the whole of creation, since he is not reckoned only to be a man like us, but also the same individual is reckoned both to be God above and to be from heaven.

ཞ Twelfth Anathema

If any do not confess that the Word of God suffered in the flesh, was crucified in the flesh, tasted death in the flesh, and became the firstborn from the dead, because as God he is both Life and the Life-giver, let them be anathema.

The Orientals' Critique

We may here, yet again, remind him of what he himself has said about the divine nature being totally devoid of suffering. In his first treatise, he wrote as follows:

The one who is more worthy than all others laid down his life for the sake of all, and for a short time he allowed his flesh to be brought low by death for the sake of the plan of salvation. But then, as Life, he destroyed death and refused to suffer anything contrary to his own nature.[129]

128. 1 Cor 15.47; Jn 3.13.
129. *Ep.* 1 (*To the Monks*) 25.

Let us say this to him in his self-contradiction: how can you first say that this individual allowed his flesh for a short time to be brought low by death and, as Life, destroyed death and refused to suffer anything contrary to his own nature, and now say that he "suffered in the flesh"? It is not the case that God suffered while attached to the flesh, but rather that the flesh, while united to God the Word, underwent its usual experiences by the Word's permission, for neither suffering nor death would happen without being allowed to. If death does not occur without permission when a soul is present, how could either suffering or death disturb his personal habitation, without permission, when God is present—and not just present, but even attached by the strongest possible union comprehensible only to himself? It is not the case that God suffered while attached to the flesh, but rather that the flesh was allowed to undergo its usual experiences. It is patently obvious that he has insidiously used this expression, "he suffered in the flesh," so as to lead simple folk astray. Someone who says that "he suffered in the flesh" can hardly be preserving the impassibility of the divine nature, since to say that "he suffered in the flesh" is exactly the equivalent of saying that "he suffered with his flesh," and if one admits this latter statement, then one has confessed him to be passible.[130] Either he suffered because he was passible by nature or else he suffered contrary to his own nature. If the former, then the Father too must be passible since he is consubstantial with the Son (since everything that is true of the begotten must be true of the begetter). Otherwise we would be confessing that the Son suffered because he was prone to do so while the Father remained apart from suffering, but if we said this we would be in agreement with the heretics who argue, from the fact that the Only-Begotten's divinity was passible while the Father's was not, that the two are therefore not consubstantial. On the other hand, if they were to argue that he suffered contrary to his own nature, we would respond by asking what kind of suffering is

130. The argument depends upon the nuances of Greek prepositions and is not transparent in English. The expression translated "in the flesh" means something like "in respect of the flesh" or "insofar as he was flesh," whereas the expression translated "with the flesh" means "together with/alongside his flesh."

so much stronger than the divine nature that it can force what is naturally impassible into suffering something contrary to its own nature. He might answer, "It was his will," and we would say, "His will is impassible, whereas we are looking for a type of suffering that can alter an impassible nature into its own form of suffering. Besides, the divine will only desires things that are appropriate for it." He will say, "What could be more appropriate than to save the human race?" And how exactly is he going to save the human race? By transforming it into a state of impassibility, or by pulling the divine and impassible nature down into suffering? The impassible is quite sufficiently strong to transform anything to its own level. What is the point of anything being passible, if even what is impassible can become passible? The salvation of the passible does not consist in its being in an association of passibility with the impassible. This would simply mean an increase of evil rather than its destruction, and passibility would likewise increase rather than being destroyed. So in what, then, does the salvation of the passible consist? It is not, as I have said, in the association of the impassible and the passible, but in the transformation of the latter by the former. What the Lord Christ did was not to bring himself, in his divinity, down to a state of suffering, but rather, by means of his holy flesh, to raise his entire humanity up to the heights, to drag what was lying on the ground up to heaven, and to make worthy of adoption what up to then had been without any freedom. What was it that was in debt to death because of its disobedience? Of course it was not the divine nature; it was the human nature. What could it possibly need to give in repayment to the death that comes from disobedience?

Cyril's Defense

The power of truth can really be relied upon, and experience is a witness too. I do not need to spend a long time defending myself on this one, or indeed explaining how those who think that I said that the Word's divine nature is passible have been deceived, once they have refuted themselves by their opposition and openly agreed that we stand wholly cleared of any charges on this point. Since they are making good use of their highly attuned intellects and are striving to demonstrate the strength of their competence by rather foolishly setting out an argument that makes them happy but which does not actually require proof, and since they are constructing an argument to prove that the Word of God is impassible in his own nature, let them therefore listen to us when we tell them that their battle is utterly futile and that they are "beating the air"[131] with nobody arrayed against them and no difference of opinion. Who would bother breaking a sweat to no purpose or stretching themselves to get something superfluous? Who would be so stupid as to describe as passible the most superior substance of all, or dare to pull what is above all becoming and is without material body down into the instability that characterizes created things? Since the very basis of the mystery is that the Only-Begotten Son, who belongs by nature to the Father, became a man for the sake of the plan of salvation, and since I affirm that the holy body that he took from the blessed Virgin actually belonged to him himself, for this very reason I can quite appropriately say that the sufferings of the flesh are called his own, in the context of his appropriating them for the sake of the plan of salvation, while always preserving the impassibility of his own nature, since he is God from God. So when we say that he suffered in the flesh, he is not reckoned to be suffering in his very own nature, insofar as he is God. Rather, he made the suffering his very own. The body that was united to him became his own, as we have just stated. This is why Paul, God's mouthpiece, said that he, the one through whom and in whom the Father made everything, became the firstborn from among the dead. This is how he put it:

… giving thanks to the Father, who has qualified us to share in the inheritance of the saints in light, who has rescued us from the dominion of darkness and brought us into the kingdom of his beloved Son, in whom we have redemption, the forgiveness of sins. This Son is the image of the invisible God, the firstborn of all creation, because in him all things were created, things in heaven and on earth, visible and invisible, whether thrones or powers or rulers or authorities; all things have been created through him and for him; and he is before all things, and

131. 1 Cor 9.26.

in him all things hold together. He is the head of the body, the church; he is the beginning and the firstborn from among the dead, so that in everything he might have the supremacy, since God was pleased to have all his fullness dwell in him, and through him to reconcile to himself all things, by making peace through the blood of his cross, whether things on earth or things in heaven.[132]

Think about how he says here that through him all things were created, visible and invisible, thrones and powers, and that he was made the head of the church, and how he insists that he became the firstborn from among the dead, and that through him he reconciled to himself all things, whether things on earth or things in heaven, and that he made peace through the blood of his cross. After this, who could possibly be in any doubt? Who could pointlessly worry that the very basis of the mystery would show the Son's nature to be passible even when it is said that he suffered in the flesh? As we have said, the sufferings that belong to the body he made his very own. This was also what Peter, that mouthpiece of God, thought appropriate, when he said, "Christ suffered for us in the flesh."[133] It is one thing to say that he suffered in the flesh, but quite another to say that the suffering was in his divine nature. Because the same individual is at the same time both God and man, impassible insofar as his divine nature is concerned, passible insofar as he is human, what is so extraordinary if one says that he suffered in respect of what is apt to suffer, while he remained impassible in respect of what does not experience suffering? The whole assembly of the holy Fathers was conspicuous for holding just this sort of belief. Let us take another look at what they have written. They were holding on to the Savior's command, remembering that he had said, "Freely you have received, so freely give."[134]

From the blessed Gregory, bishop of Nyssa:

"May you have the same attitude as did Christ Jesus, who, although he was in God's form, did not intend to grasp at equality with God; instead he emptied himself by taking the form of a servant."[135] What could be poorer when compared to God than the form of a servant? What could be more humiliating for the Ruler of the universe than willingly

---

132. Col 1.12–20.
134. Mt 10.8.

133. 1 Pt 4.1.
135. Phil 2.5–7.

to enter into an association with our impoverished nature? The King of kings and Lord of lords donned the form of a servant. The Judge of all became a taxpayer to the authorities. The Lord of creation descended into a cave. The one who held the universe in his hand could find no room at the inn and was cast into a feeding trough for animals. The one who was wholly pure accepted sordid human nature and, by passing through extreme poverty, even entered into the trial of death. Look at the extent of his voluntary impoverishment. Life itself tasted death. The Judge was led into a court. The Lord of all living things submitted to the decree of a magistrate. The King of all transcendent power did not disdain the hands of common men.[136]

From Basil, bishop of Caesarea:

For even heaven and earth and the great seas, even the creatures that live in the water and on the dry land, even the plants, the stars, the air, and the seasons, even the vast variety in the order of the universe do not display God's transcendent power nearly as well as does the fact that God, although he is incomprehensible, was able, impassibly, through flesh, to have come into close conflict with death, so that by his own suffering he might bestow impassibility upon us.[137]

From Athanasius, bishop of Alexandria:

He showed that he had a body, not in appearance, but in truth. It was appropriate for the Lord, when he put on human flesh, to put it on whole, together with the sufferings proper to it; so that, just as we say that the body belonged to him himself, so we may also say that the body's sufferings belonged to him himself, even though they did not touch him as far as his divinity was concerned. If then the body had been another's, then the sufferings would have been attributed to him; but if the flesh is the Word's (for "the Word became flesh"), then the sufferings of the flesh must also be said to belong to him, whose the flesh is. And the one to whom the sufferings are ascribed, such things as being condemned, being scourged, thirsting, the cross, death, and the other infirmities of the body, his also are the triumph and the grace. This is why it is consistent and fitting that such sufferings are not ascribed to someone else, but to the Lord; that the grace may also be from him so that we do not become man-worshipers, but that we be genuinely devoted to God, because we do not call upon anything that came into existence or upon any ordinary man, but upon the natural, genuine Son of God, the very one who became a man, yet is not thereby any the less Lord and God and Savior.[138]

136. Gregory of Nyssa, *On the Beatitudes* 1 (PG 44:1201B).
137. Basil, *De Spiritu Sancto* 8.18.
138. Athanasius, *Contra Arianos* 3.32.

These citations are quite sufficient, I reckon, to make the point to sensible folk, since the divine Scripture is quite explicit that "every saying shall be established on the testimony of two or three witnesses."[139] If anyone still wants to argue about this, then let him listen to me: he has gone off by himself; I am the one who is stating the truth and keeping in line with both the sacred Scriptures and the faith of the holy Fathers. I am thereby winning the prize of the heavenward calling in Christ,[140] through whom and with whom be glory to our God and Father, together with the Holy Spirit, forever and ever. Amen.

139. Dt 19.15.
140. Cf. Phil 3.14.

INDICES

GENERAL INDEX

Aaron, 119, 164
Abraham, 42, 46, 48, 61, 78, 97, 101, 109, 124, 139, 140, 142, 145
adoptionism, 10, 12
Alexander of Hierapolis, 6
alteration, 30, 44, 85, 89–90, 121, 178
Amphilochius of Iconium, 106, 138
Andrew of Samosata, 6, 7, 8, 14, 15, 16, 17, 18, 19, 20, 21, 22, 23, 24, 25, 135, 136, 139, 152, 155, 171
Apollinarianism, 10, 13, 22, 24–26, 51, 53, 56, 66, 126–27, 143
Apollinarius of Laodicaea, 19, 22, 40, 84, 139, 146, 151, 156
appearance, 43, 47, 58, 101, 136, 175, 181
Arianism, 8, 10, 12, 20, 46, 99, 102, 144, 146
Aristotle, 17–18, 52, 97, 161
assumed flesh/body, 40–41, 67, 74, 141, 170
Athanasius, 11, 22, 25, 39, 137, 156, 157, 175, 181
Atticism, 29
Atticus of Constantinople, 150

baptism, 68, 72–73, 79, 102, 121, 130, 136, 142
Basil of Caesarea, 21, 25, 106, 139, 181
begotten, 16, 39, 41, 44, 48–50, 60, 71, 86, 103, 105, 122–23, 129, 134, 137–38, 142, 145, 156, 177
blending, 30–31, 144

Celestine (pope), 5, 9
Chalcedon, 17, 26, 77
change, 12, 14, 16, 21, 25, 30, 44–45, 78, 85, 89–90, 93, 98, 102, 105–6,

108, 113–14, 118, 121, 128, 133, 135–37, 140, 165, 167, 176
Chrysostom, 6, 106
combination (of natures), 8, 31, 52, 60–61, 102
complete humanity, 13, 40, 53
composition (of natures), 8, 19, 51–52, 68, 77, 82, 84, 108, 158–59
concrete existence (*hypostasis*), 17, 18, 23, 30–31, 40, 47–49, 58–59, 89, 91–95, 98–99, 138–39, 141–44, 149–51, 153, 158, 161–62
concurrence (of natures), 31, 51, 60, 67
confusion, 17, 18, 30–31, 67, 72, 75, 90, 92, 93, 102, 104, 125, 127, 133, 137, 143, 157, 165, 166, 171–72, 173, 176
conjoining (of natures), 31, 64–65, 75, 89
connection (of natures), 7–8, 18, 31, 91, 93–96, 98, 114, 120, 125, 126, 138, 142, 157, 170, 171
Constantinople, 4, 5, 140, 150
consubstantiality, 60, 86, 100, 142, 162–63, 170, 173, 177
converging (of natures), 18, 31, 51–53, 63, 90, 94, 96, 98, 105, 138
Council of Ephesus, first (431 CE), 3–4, 6, 7, 8, 9, 11, 17, 20, 26–27, 83, 99, 150, 153
Council of Ephesus, second (449 CE), 11

David, 42, 45, 54, 56, 60–61, 79, 82, 85, 92, 101, 105, 119, 120–23, 125–26, 129, 137, 140, 145, 164, 166, 169
Diodore, 5, 12, 19, 23

185

INDEX OF HOLY SCRIPTURE

RECENT VOLUMES IN THE
FATHERS OF THE CHURCH SERIES

WORKS OF ST. CYRIL OF ALEXANDRIA
IN THIS SERIES

Letters 1–50, translated by John I. McEnerney,
Fathers of the Church 76 (1987)

Letters 51–110, translated by John I. McEnerney,
Fathers of the Church 77 (1987)

Commentary on the Twelve Prophets, Volume 1, translated by
Robert C. Hill, Fathers of the Church 115 (2007)

Commentary on the Twelve Prophets, Volume 2, translated by
†Robert C. Hill, Fathers of the Church 116 (2008)

Commentary on the Twelve Prophets, Volume 3, translated by
†Robert C. Hill, Fathers of the Church 124 (2012)

Festal Letters 1–12, translated by Philip R. Amidon, SJ, and
edited with introduction and notes by John J. O'Keefe,
Fathers of the Church 118 (2009)

Festal Letters 13–30, translated by Philip R. Amidon, SJ,
and edited with notes by John J. O'Keefe,
Fathers of the Church 127 (2013)

Three Christological Treatises, translated by Daniel King,
Fathers of the Church 129 (2014)

MUSKINGUM COLLEGE LIBRARY

3 8152 002 236 557

GAYLORD

MUSKINGUM UNIVERSITY LIBRARY

163 STORMONT STREET
NEW CONCORD, OHIO 43762